Best Hikes With
CHILDREN
in Arizona

Best Hikes With
CHILDREN®
in Arizona

By Lawrence Letham

THE
MOUNTAINEERS

*To the memory of my parents, Daryl and
Joan Letham, and the scout leaders of my youth,
Hugh L. Sharp and Robert T. Roberts.*

 Published by
The Mountaineers
1001 SW Klickitat Way, Suite 201
Seattle, WA 98134

Published simultaneously in Great Britain by Cordee, 3a DeMontfort Street,
Leicester, England, LE1 7HD

Manufactured in the United States of America

Edited by Kris Fulsaas
Maps and photography by Lawrence Letham
All photographs by Lawrence Letham
Cover design by Watson Graphics
Book layout by Ani Rucki
Cover photograph: *Children enjoying Red Rock country near Sedona*
Frontispiece: *The spectacular multicolored cliffs of the Grand Canyon*
Title page: *Tall rocks near Betatakin Ruins*

Library of Congress Cataloging-in-Publication Data
Letham, Lawrence.
    Best hikes with children in Arizona / by Lawrence Letham.—1st
ed.
        p.   cm.
    Includes bibliographical references.
    ISBN 0-89886-515-8
    1. Hiking—Arizona—Guidebooks. 2. Family recreation—Arizona—
Guidebooks. 3. Trails—Arizona—Guidebooks. 4. Arizona—
Guidebooks. I. Title.
GV199.42.A7L48   1998
917.9104'53—dc21   97-44974
                                                           CIP

Contents

Map Legend

Symbol	Meaning	Symbol	Meaning
❬	Gate	▲	Mountain Peak
Ⓢ	Trail Start	×	Point of Interest
Ⓟ	Parking		Canyon Rim or Cliff Edge
Ⓡ	Rest room		
⏧	Turnaround	⛺	Campground/Campsite
■	Building	⛩	Picnic Site
◙	Viewpoint		
———	Dirt Road	N	North
——	Road	⛏	Mine
—··—	Hiking Route (Asphalt)	○	City
– – – –	Hiking Route (Dirt)	⬆	Entrance Gate/Ranger Station/ Park Office
··········	Other Trail		
˙·˙·˙·˙	Dry Stream or Wash	⬯	Interstate Highway
～～	River or Stream	⬯	US Highway
⬤	Lake or Pond	◯	State Highway
)(	Pass	☐	Forest Road

Acknowledgments

Thanks to my wife and children for their patience and for joining me on these hikes. Thank you to all of the managing agencies that provided valuable information, interesting insights, and assistance.

Bizarre saguaro is a unique find along the trail.

Little hiker investigating plants along the trail

Introduction

When I was young, my parents did not engage in many outdoor activities, but that does not mean that I did not hike a lot. I remember walking miles through museums, historical landmarks, and other city-oriented adventures. We covered a lot of ground.

My interest in the outdoors was sparked when I became a Boy Scout at the age of twelve. I hiked, camped, built fires, and learned to love the outdoors. It is a love that I work to pass on to my own children, so that they too can feel the awe and gratitude inspired by nature. They still get to see the museums, but those trips are packed in between outdoor adventures. Hiking with my children is more than just a fun time; we grow closer together and share memories that none of us will ever forget. It is also satisfying to hear them recount how much fun they had on an outing and ask to do it again.

Children on the Trail

The most important goal to accomplish when hiking with your children is to enjoy the experience, but age determines what is enjoyable. Young children, between three and five years old, want to touch everything they see. They are not very interested in a beautiful view or an amazing landscape. Touching a blade of grass is far more satisfying to them than reaching a destination or seeing anything in the distance. Older children want to touch things too, but they also want to get someplace. Most children between six and ten years old are capable of strenuous hikes. They want to see things and reach destinations, but they do not comprehend the spectacular qualities of many of the views, probably because they have not seen enough of nature to know, comparatively, what is unique.

The hikes in this book have been chosen to offer elements of interest to children of all ages. The most important aspect is the things that children can touch or see up close. Concentrate on finding items to look at next to the trail, whether it be ants, pretty rocks, or a pack rat's bite marks in a prickly pear cactus. Encourage your children to show you the things they like and find fascinating. Allow them to explore and touch, but not to destroy or collect.

Keeping Children Interested

When hiking with children of disparate ages, the smaller ones may tire and lose interest while the older ones want to press on to reach a destination. You cannot always limit the hike to appeal to only the younger children, or the older children may lose interest. Be positive and use some of the techniques listed below to keep children's interest. The overall goal is to have fun and enjoy each other's company while also enjoying nature. The activities listed below can help children enjoy the experience as they learn to hike and love the outdoors.

Singing a song: Singing is one of the easiest diversions available. If you and your children do not know any songs, learn some. Any songs that you enjoy will do, but those that have hand actions are even better for the little children.

Blindfolded walk: The person who is blindfolded is guided down the trail by verbal instructions. This is a good game for relatively flat stretches, but it does slow the pace.

Identification: With eyes closed, the person identifies whatever is placed in his or her hands.

Find tinder: The person finds tinder for making a fire in the field. Finding tinder in the desert can be challenging, and once it is found, there is usually nothing more to burn, but it helps children be more observant.

I spy: One person thinks of something that everyone can see, and gives a clue such as "I spy something round and hard." The others try to guess what it is.

Twenty questions: A person thinks of some object or person. The other players ask yes-or-no questions to deduce the nature of the object. This activity is good for many miles with the older children.

Where was that?: After walking for several minutes, ask children about the order of the things you passed. How much do they really remember?

How far?: Have each person guess how far they have hiked. For older children, show them how to orient the map and locate your position.

Cloud pictures: Look into the sky and describe to each other what you see in the clouds.

Chain story: One person starts a story, but stops in the middle of a sentence or idea. The next person must continue the story, then break to let the next person carry on, and so forth.

Yes or no: A person can ask any question of any other person, but the words "yes" or "no" cannot be used in any of the answers. Actually, any words can be prohibited. It makes children think before they speak.

Name a class: Have a person name all the presidents of the United States that they can think of, or all the baseball players, et cetera.

Enjoying Nature

If hiking is introduced to children in the right way, they will love it. Start with having a positive attitude yourself, then follow the suggestions below to get children ready to enjoy what can become a lifelong activity.

Build anticipation: Children get excited when they anticipate something fun. Getting ready the night before really gets children ready to go. Tell them the exciting things they will see or any well-known events that occurred at the location.

Allow exploring: Whenever there is something interesting or new to see, take the time to explore it. If you cannot get to the end of the trail because time was spent watching ants carry food back to the nest, do not worry. When it is time to go back, simply turn around wherever you are and return. The same trail can be hiked to the end another time. Enjoy watching your children experience the thrill of discovery.

There is one note of caution. Some of the wilderness parks in Arizona are preserves. There are strict laws protecting artifacts, flora, and fauna. Hikers may also be restricted to the established

Geological training starts early.

trails. When you do not have to stay on the trail, be sure that all explorations leave the area in the same, or better, condition than you found it. Never collect artifacts, not even twigs, branches, or rocks. Leave everything as it was for the next person to enjoy just as much as you did.

Lots of praise: Right from the beginning of the hike, children need to hear how well they are doing. They need lots of praise and positive reinforcement. Look for specific examples of good work to praise, such as helping with the smaller children, staying on the trail, having a good stride, and choosing a good spot to rest. Praise makes children want to go on the next hike because of the positive experiences they have every time they go.

Scenic views: Stop for scenic views and explain why they are beautiful. It helps children develop a feel for the wonders that can be seen only outdoors. It is also worth the effort to carry a camera. Take a picture of everyone with the view in the background. It will be a reminder of a wonderful trip.

Pace: The answer to the question "What is the best pace?" has to be determined by each family. Most children want to take off running at the beginning of the hike and are soon exhausted. A pace must be set that slows the leaders when they are fresh and keeps everyone going when they are tired. Except at scenic views, take short, standing rest breaks, so the regular pace is not broken, but watch for signs of exhaustion. If the adults or children are dragging their feet, are slow to restart after a break, or whine a lot, they are too tired and are not enjoying anything. If you and your children have not hiked very much, start with short, easy trails, so you can feel the accomplishment of completing the hike without overexerting yourselves. As your endurance increases, so will your ability to go longer and farther.

Leader and anchor: A technique for managing the hike is to assign a leader and an anchor. The leader sets the pace and shows the way. The anchor is the last person in the group. Anchors make sure that no one is left behind, so they have to be responsible people, preferably an adult.

At the beginning of the hike when everyone is fresh, put the slowest person in front. Later on when everyone is tired, put a stronger hiker as the leader. The other children will work hard to keep up, so a good pace will be maintained. Just so nobody gets lost, do not let children get too far ahead; it is better to keep them in sight.

On some hikes, nothing you do will keep the younger hikers going. Either there is too much to touch and explore or it is just an off day. Do not get frustrated. The primary objective is to enjoy the experience, so be flexible about the pace and how far you go.

Distance: The length of a hike that children can accomplish and enjoy depends on their age, health, and strength. As you hike with

*The many box canyons of the Colorado Plateau provide scenic
views of both desert and forest.*

your children, you will learn their limits; however, do not push them
to their limits until they really like hiking, or they may not want to
go again. On a long hike that the older children can easily accomplish,
prepare in advance to carry the younger children if you really want
to go the entire distance. Also, leave extra time to rest just in case
the hike is harder than you anticipated.

Electronics: Technology has made it possible to have electronic
entertainment anyplace in the world at any time of day, but that is
not what hiking is all about. Children need experiences on the trail
that they cannot get elsewhere. A tape recorder, CD player, television,
or video game focuses their attention on something they can get at
home. They will miss the adventure because their minds are focused
on the electronic entertainment. Make it a rule that none of that stuff
even gets into the car. The only exceptions might be a cellular tele-
phone, because it is indispensable in a pinch, and a Global Positioning
System (GPS) receiver, because it can add a new dimension to the
hike. Both children and adults are fascinated by the GPS because
their position on the receiver's screen moves as they move. It also

provides a visual representation of where you are, where you have been, and how much farther you have to go.

Snacks: Food gives energy to working bodies, so it is an important part of a hike. There are excellent snacks that are high in energy yet lightweight: dried meats or fruits, hard candy, hard cheese, nuts, grapes, granola bars, cookies, and firm breads like bagels that can take the abuse of a backpack. Try out new snacks before the hike, so you know whether your children will eat them.

Environmental Etiquette

No-trace hiking is the only way to preserve the outdoors for future generations. It is disappointing to visit one of your favorite destinations only to find that it has been vandalized or filled with litter. The only hope we have of preserving nature is for parents to teach their children to treat the outdoors with respect, so the destruction not only stops, but begins to be reversed. Children by their nature want to do what is right; they just need to be taught. As adults we have to be careful not to say one thing and do another, because children follow example more readily than words. The following are just a few of the things we can teach our children to help them grow to be responsible adults.

Respect for Private Property

Some of the wilderness areas of Arizona are accessible via private land or Indian reservations. Respect for private property is important to maintain access. Many of the public lands are also multiple-use areas, so it is not unusual to see livestock, water tanks, or corrals far from civilization. Some trails that lie entirely on Indian reservations or private preserves require permits. The description for each hike specifies where to obtain permits, if necessary. Teach your children to never destroy anything that is not their own, and they will learn to care for property regardless of ownership.

Conservation

Leave an area better than you found it. Teach your children to hike and camp so that there is no trace that they were ever there. By way of example and gentle reminders, teach your children to stay on the trail, to leave the plants alone, to not throw rocks, to care properly for fires, and other good outdoor manners. They will learn to be responsible even when no one is looking.

Bathroom Stops

Many of the trailheads in this book have bathrooms available, but just in case the inevitable happens on the trail, always carry some toilet paper. Select a spot that is at least 200 feet from the trail and any water source, and dig a hole 4 to 6 inches deep. Pack out toilet paper with you like any other trash. Sometimes in the desert it is difficult to find a stick to dig a hole, so carry a small garden trowel in your backpack.

Safety

Hopefully, you will never experience any type of an emergency during a hike; however, just in case the unexpected happens, it is important to be prepared. Knowing how to handle situations that may arise inspires confidence and eliminates fear, and there may even be opportunities to help people who are less well-prepared. Some important areas of preparation are listed below.

First Aid

Carry a small first-aid kit that is readily accessible. Know how to deal with minor cuts, blisters, broken limbs, and sprains. A few books that deal with first aid in the outdoors are listed in the Suggested Reading at the back of this book. Keep a larger first-aid kit in your vehicle to supplement the supplies of the portable one. In the desert, carry tweezers or pliers to remove cactus spines.

No-trace hiking preserves fascinating ruins for future generations.

Water

Always plan to carry all the water you will need. Unfortunately, water's weight is heavy for little children, so it is important to know how much is really necessary. In the desert, one gallon per person per day is the minimum; one gallon of water weighs about eight pounds. At higher, cooler elevations, one-half gallon per person per day will suffice. Older children and adults will have to carry water for the smaller children.

In some areas, there are streams and springs that can provide water, but it must be purified by a method that removes the *Giardia lamblia* cyst. In the desert, never depend on water from a spring or any other natural source even if it is mentioned in the hike description. Water sources are seasonal and probably will not be there when you need them the most.

To monitor children's water intake in order to be sure that they are getting enough, have a separate canteen for each child, and instruct them not to share. Make sure everyone takes frequent drinks to keep from dehydrating. If the hike is on a hot Arizonan day, freeze the water in the canteens the night before so the water is cool for the entire trip.

Hypothermia

If the body's core temperature drops below normal, 98.6° Fahrenheit, the condition is known as hypothermia; if left untreated, it is deadly. Advanced symptoms of hypothermia are incoherent speech, cold skin, disorientation, or listlessness. When children start whining or are uncooperative, make sure they are warm. If they are not, take immediate action to get them dry and warm. It is impossible for victims of hypothermia to recognize the symptoms in themselves, so watch each other carefully.

Hypothermia strikes in surprising conditions. A case in Arizona occurred when a woman was fishing on a warm day. The sky clouded over, the temperature dropped quickly, and it rained before she could take cover. Because the storm was brief and it did not seem cold, she did not take any action. In wet clothes at about 50° Fahrenheit, her body temperature could not keep up and she developed hypothermia. Fortunately, her partner recognized the symptoms and helped her.

The right clothing helps to keep you warm. Take rain gear and find shelter when it rains. Avoid being wet from sweat by wearing clothing in layers. When you are hot, remove layers and as you cool down, put more back on. Choose clothing based on its material. Cotton does not retain warmth when it gets wet, but wool, cotton-polyester blends, silk, and polypropylene retain heat even when soaked. A hat,

A log bench offers quiet repose at the end of the trail.

gloves, and warm shoes are also important in cold weather because most of the body's heat is lost through the extremities.

Hypothermia is not a problem in the lower-elevation deserts during the summer because the nighttime low temperatures are too high. However, there are areas of the state at higher altitudes where it gets cold at night regardless of the time of year. During the monsoon season it can rain unexpectedly, so be prepared with the proper clothing.

Hyperthermia

Hyperthermia, also known as heat exhaustion and heat stroke, is the opposite condition of hypothermia. When the body gets hot, it sweats to try to maintain a stable temperature. If the water lost through perspiration is not replaced, the body's temperature rises and makes the person sick.

Watch children for the symptoms of heat exhaustion: dizziness, pale face, weakness, listlessness, or nausea. If the symptoms appear, put the person in the shade, have him or her lie down, and give sips of water every 10 to 15 minutes until the person feels better. To prevent hyperthermia, make sure children drink regularly even if they say they are not thirsty, because simply satisfying your thirst does not necessarily replace all the water lost through sweat.

Heat stroke is an acute case of heat exhaustion and is a medical emergency. The symptoms are headache, nausea, skin that is hot and dry (dry because the body has stopped sweating), fever, red face, or even unconsciousness. While waiting to evacuate the person for medical treatment, have him or her lie down in the shade while you cool his or her body with water or ice. If conscious, give sips of water that has a bit of salt in it to replace the salt the person has lost through sweating. Get medical attention for the person soon.

The desert can get so hot that sweat evaporates before your clothes get wet, so do not be fooled into thinking that you are not being affected by the heat. A warm day or hard hiking means you are losing water even if there is not any dripping perspiration. In the hot summer months, either stop hiking in the desert or restrict your activities to the cooler, early morning hours.

Getting Lost or Stranded

Every year in Arizona there is at least one death from exposure to the intense summer heat. Lack of water while walking in the hot sun leads to heat stroke, then death. It is not enough to teach your children to stay in one place when they are lost—they need to get out of the sun and then wait. If the car breaks down, regardless of the

Granite boulders formed from magma that did not erupt from a volcano, but seeped to the surface.

proximity of the highway, wait until the sun goes down before walking out. Better yet, just wait until the rescue crew arrives at the car. Always tell someone at home where you are going and when you should get back. It is best to leave them a copy of the map of the intended trail.

Flash Floods

It does not rain often in the desert, but when it does, the water runoff can cause dangerous flash floods. The desert soil is so dry that it takes a while before it can absorb the rain. The water from a hard rain quickly turns dry washes and gullies into fierce rivers. Never cross, even in a car, a wash that has running water in it. The water is always dirty from the soil it carries, so it is impossible to determine its depth and the currents are deceptively strong. Wait until the water flow dies down before crossing.

Venomous Animals

The probability of even seeing a gila monster, scorpion, black widow spider, brown recluse spider, or poisonous snake is extremely low, and the chances of being bitten by one are even lower. It is more likely that a person will be struck by lightning than bitten by a poisonous animal, and even if there is a chance meeting, the creature will be just as afraid of you as you are of it. If it is left alone, everything will be fine. In the very, very rare case that someone is bitten or stung, it is time to end the hike and get back to medical facilities quickly. General first-aid procedures for different kinds of poisonous bites and stings are given below. Expert advice can always be obtained from the Arizona Poison Control Center, whose toll-free phone number is (800) 362-0101.

Scorpions. If you or your child is stung by a scorpion, find it, if possible, for identification, then end your trip and get back to medical attention. Do not panic, but put ice or something cold on the sting and start back to the car. Each person's reaction to a scorpion sting is different. Most times it will just swell and hurt for a few hours; however, if the symptoms of poisoning appear—headaches, difficulty in walking, blurred vision, and slurred speech—get the person to a hospital soon to receive the anti-venom.

There is no reason to be afraid of scorpions, but take simple precautions to avoid being stung: wear shoes, shake out your sleeping bag before you get in it and your shoes before you put them on, look before you sit, and never put your bare hands in a bush or under a rock.

Spiders. Another unlikely, but possible, event is to be bitten by a spider. There are no first-aid procedures for spider bites aside from washing the area with soap and water. If someone is bitten, capture the spider, if possible, for identification and get to medical attention as soon as possible. The same precautions taken to avoid scorpion stings should be used to protect against spider bites. Spiders are not aggressive and will bite only when molested.

Gila monster. The chance of being bitten by the colorful gila (pronounced *HE-la*) monster is extremely rare. If you see one, stay back and no one will be hurt. When gila monsters bite, they clamp their jaws shut and hang on. Pry it off by putting a stick in its mouth or by pulling on its tail. Allow the wound to bleed unless bleeding is profuse, immobilize the limb, and get medical attention.

Snakes. Snake bites are also very rare, but they are serious. The two most common poisonous snakes in Arizona are coral snakes and rattlesnakes. Coral snakes will always try to get away unless they are harassed, and rattlesnakes will give a warning with their rattles when you approach. Take the same precautions listed above for scorpions to also avoid snakes. It is always wise to stay on the trail because bushwhacking puts you right into the snakes' habitat. Also, do not collect firewood after dark or get too close when identifying a snake. If by chance someone is bitten, keep the victim calm, immobilize the area of the bite, and transport the person to medical help.

What to Take

Packs

Backpacks are important for carrying water, food, clothes, and other equipment for a hike. Older children need well-built backpacks that are comfortable under a load, because they help carry most of the essentials, especially water, for the younger children. If you have backpacks for younger children, even if they are school backpacks or play ones, take them along and let the small children carry something light.

A good backpack is one that fits and is padded appropriately for the load. A pack for a day hike does not need a frame, but a waist belt helps to transfer some of the load to the hips. A nice feature in a backpack is side pockets to hold water bottles for quick access, so you do not have to dig through the pack every time you need a drink.

Also available are child-carrier backpacks, which carry small children. Look for one that is comfortable for both passenger and carrier. Some come with detachable roofs to protect the child from sun and rain. There also needs to be a way to carry equipment in addition to the child. Some backpacks come with compartments that attach to the frame and hold more equipment, but it is also possible to just attach your own backpack under the child's seat.

Footwear

A good pair of hiking boots provide support on rough terrain, but boots can be expensive, especially considering that children's feet grow so fast. If the hike is easy and relatively flat, a pair of sneakers will do fine. But on a longer hike with more elevation change and rocks in the trail, boots are important. Features to look for are lightweight, stiff soles, and high ankles. High-top sneakers are a good alternative, but they usually are not as sturdy as good boots.

Clothing

Clothing is the first line of defense against the elements. Skin cancer is one of the most prevalent cancers in the United States, and Arizona leads the nation in cases of skin cancer only because people do not take the proper precautions. Whether you are in the desert or the mountains, protect yourself and your children from the sun. Where the clothing does not cover, use sunscreen. Long pants make sense at any time because they protect from the sun and against scrapes and cuts from trailside brush and cacti.

Clothing for the desert should be lightweight, but in spring and fall be prepared with extra clothing for the cool mornings and nights. In the mountains, dress in layers so when it gets cold you can add layers and when you get hot, you can remove some. Do not make the mistake of not taking enough warm clothing when going from the hot desert to the higher elevations. Sometimes desert dwellers forget that it actually gets uncomfortably cold in other parts of Arizona. During the monsoon season and the winter, always be prepared for rain in the deserts or snow in the mountains.

Food

The foremost rule to food is: if the children do not like it, do not take it. Always choose healthy foods that provide energy, but that the children also enjoy.

An important issue about trail food is the level of effort needed to prepare it. If you like to cook outdoors, you will need a camping stove, pans, utensils, etc. If you do not want to carry all that equipment on the trail, cooking can be done at the car before or after the hike. If you want delicious, hot food on the trail, lightweight backpacking stoves make it possible. Food preparation can range from opening a package to eat prepared food, to heating something up, to cooking from scratch. Once you decide the amount of energy and time you want to spend cooking, choose food that the children really like.

Any food you carry on the trail should be lightweight. Dehydrated foods should be chosen over canned foods because of the difference in weight. Repackaging food into single servings makes it easier to divide up for carrying and to use on the trail. Snacks also play an important part of nutrition on the trail (see Enjoying Nature, earlier in the Introduction).

The Ten Essentials

There are ten items that are considered essential on a hike of any length or duration. The list was developed over the years by The Mountaineers to help prepare you to deal with the unexpected.

1. **Extra clothes:** Taking extra clothes ensures that children are warm and protected and can enjoy the hike. It can get chilly in the desert at night and positively cold at higher elevations. It may be warm during the day, but as the sun descends, the temperature falls rapidly.

2. **Extra food:** A child's mood depends a lot on his or her stomach. If children are hungry, they are a lot less cooperative. In addition to the planned menu, take additional high-energy food. It will be important if the hike is a little harder or longer than expected.

3. **Sunglasses/hat:** Both sunglasses and a hat are important in the desert, where there is little or no protection from the scorching sun. In the woods, the sunglasses may not be needed, but the hat is important in case of inclement weather. A baseball cap shades the eyes, but it does not provide much protection when it rains, nor does it shield the neck or ears from the sun. A hat with a brim around the entire circumference is better; if all you have are baseball caps, they will do if you put sunscreen on all the other body parts exposed to the sun. If you carry a small baby in a carrier, be sure that he or she is shielded from the sun with either a hat or something that attaches to the carrier itself.

4. **Pocket knife:** A good knife is indispensable. It can cut food, whittle sticks for tinder to start fires, saw branches, open cans, and be used for a host of other tasks, depending on its blades. A knife that includes tweezers to remove cactus spines is also nice. Survival tools that include pliers are also useful for dealing with cactus spines.

5. **Firestarter:** If you ever get stuck outdoors, it is important to be able to build a fire to provide warmth and security. There is a plethora of fire-starting materials: fire sticks, fire paste, candles in a can, steel wool, or lint from your clothes dryer. Some are easier to use than others, so practice making a few fires to know which is best for you.

6. **First-aid kit:** Carry a first-aid kit and know how to use it. See the first-aid discussion under the section Safety earlier in the Introduction.

7. **Matches:** Matches light campfires, campstoves, or lanterns. Always

carry a couple of books of matches in your backpack for general use and keep the "strike-anywhere," wooden matches in a waterproof container for emergencies. Commercially prepared waterproof matches are also available.

8. **Flashlight:** It is worth it to purchase a small, high-powered flashlight that runs on two AA batteries and has a beam that can be focused. Put fresh batteries in it before the trip, and carry one set of spares. Some flashlights can even hold a spare bulb in the cap at the end. Candle lanterns are nice in camp when light in all directions is needed, but they are less useful when the light must be focused on a trail in the dark.

9. **Map:** It is important to carry a map of the area just in case you get lost. Know how to use it and, in the case of a topographical map, how to read the topological symbols. Learning to use a map is easy and adds a new dimension to the hike. In the desert where everything can look the same, it takes real skill to determine your location on the map.

10. **Compass:** Knowledge of how to use a compass is necessary to use a map. In most hikes in this book, you do not need to use a topographical map or compass, but at a trail intersection, a properly oriented map makes it easier to take the right trail.

Arizona

Arizona is an outdoor enthusiast's dream. The terrain ranges from the Painted Desert to heavy conifer forests along with high mountains, sheer cliffs, sand dunes, and even meteor craters. There is an abundance of lakes, most of them man-made, and many of them are surrounded by the steep mountains whose valleys were filled when the dams were built. Plants of all varieties dot the terrain and add splashes of color to green forests and vast deserts. Best of all is the weather. Most of the state enjoys more than 300 days of clear skies and sunshine every year.

There are also thousands of miles of established trails on over 30 million acres of public lands. Some trails lead to the peaks of mountains with spectacular views while others meander through forests, weird rock formations, cactus gardens, streams, Indian ruins, ghost towns, and even the colossal Grand Canyon. Hikers who live in metropolitan areas do not even have to travel far to enjoy the outdoors. Many trails are found right in the Phoenix area where city and county governments have developed large, beautiful preserves of many thousands of acres.

Great weather, beautiful scenery, and trails of all levels of challenge make the Arizona outdoors so enticing that it is impossible to resist. Get your children and go. They will love you forever for taking them to see what the great Arizona outdoors has to offer.

Life Zones

There are six distinct life zones in Arizona. The climate and altitude determine the plant and animal life of each zone.

Lower Sonoran Life Zone: In the southwest portion of Arizona is the hot, arid desert that receives a maximum of 12 inches of rain between July to September and December to February. It starts at 100 feet and continues to 3,500 feet in altitude. It is too dry to support grasses, but there are many small-leafed bushes like creosote, mesquite, paloverde, brittlebush, bursage, and Joshua tree. All varieties of cacti like saguaro, cholla, prickly pear, organ pipe, and barrel cactus live throughout the area. Animals in the hot desert include the white-tailed deer, desert bighorn sheep, coyote, rabbits, a variety of snakes, lizards, spiders, and scorpions. Birds of prey are frequently seen soaring high overhead. The peccary, better known as the javelina, is a pig-like animal that eats the prickly pear cacti, spines and all. Although the desert may look barren, it is a wonderland to the careful observer.

Upper Sonoran Life Zone: The next zone lies between 3,500 and 7,000 feet, primarily in the state's northeast corner. It too is an arid region, but it is a cold desert that receives between 7 and 22 inches of annual rainfall. There are grasses, sagebrush, scrub oak, manzanita, and even trees like junipers, pinyon, and oak. Along the banks of streams, riparian trees such as cottonwood, willows, and walnut are common. Even though the area is a desert, there are few cacti because of the cold temperatures. Deer, porcupines, black bear, rabbits, and gray fox are common in this zone, as well as in some of the higher zones.

Transition Life Zone: The ponderosa pine tree is the predominate plant of the life zone that occurs between 7,000 and 8,000 feet. The Kaibab Plateau, near the Grand Canyon, and the Mogollon Rim, a cliff-like ridge that crosses the entire state, are good examples of the Transition Life Zone; however, it also occurs on mountains in any part of the state that reach that altitude and receive no less than 18 inches of rain per year. There are also plants like buckbrush, manzanita, and even hedgehog cactus. Elk are found in this life zone.

Canadian Life Zone: The Douglas fir and white fir trees found in this life zone grow 150 feet high and live between 200 and 400 years. The zone, stretching to altitudes of between 8,000 and 9,000 feet, receives approximately 25 inches of rain per year and has other plants like Gambel oak, aspen, grasses, and some shrubs.

Hudsonian Life Zone: This life zone, between 9,000 and 11,500 feet, supports primarily spruce and alpine fir trees.

The hardy plant life of the Upper Sonoran Life Zone can survive in any terrain.

Arctic-Alpine Life Zone: This is found above tree line at 11,500 feet and higher. In Arizona this zone is found only on the upper reaches of the San Franciscan Peaks near Flagstaff. The trees at timberline are twisted by strong winds and heavy snows, while their growth is stunted by poor soil conditions. The plants above tree line are of an arctic variety like moss, lichens, and grasses. The tundra pipit, a bird, is the only animal that makes its home in such a hostile environment.

The Big Cacti

There are two Arizonan plants that merit discussion in particular: the saguaro (pronounced *suh-WAR-oh*) and the organ pipe cactus. In the United States, the giant saguaro is found only in Arizona and a tiny strip of desert in California. The majority of the U.S. distribution of the organ pipe cactus is limited to the small area of Organ Pipe Cactus National Monument. These two cacti are unique and impressive.

The saguaro cactus lives upwards of 150 to 200 years. A full-grown saguaro is about 40 feet tall and weighs several tons, yet its growth is amazingly slow. Depending on the climate and soil, it can take from between 5 and 10 years for a saguaro to grow the first inch. Most plants are 12 feet after 50 years and 30 feet after 100 years. It is not until age 65 that the cactus starts growing branches, which are referred to as arms. The arms usually grow out from the body, then up toward the sky, making cacti with two arms look a lot like a person being held up by a bandit. Regardless of age or size, saguaro cacti are easily identified by their lengthwise pleats. The saguaro is protected from theft and vandalism by strict state laws. Although it grows over a large part of the state, the best place to see thousands of them is in Saguaro National Monument near Tucson.

The organ pipe cactus looks a lot like its name. From a single root, a multitude of slender branches shoot straight into the air and can withstand the abuse of 118° Fahrenheit heat with very little water. Like any other cacti, they are susceptible to freezing during the winter, so their distributions are greatest on the south side of slopes, where the winter sun warms them. They bloom sometime between May and July, but their blossoms only open when it is cooler at night.

Weather

Arizona's different climatic regions allow people to choose the weather they want to enjoy during their trip. In the summer, the temperature is scorching in the desert, but the days are cool in the mountains. Winter brings snow to higher elevations and enjoyable days to the desert, so hikers can have it all, usually whenever they want it— though there are bound to be some storms occasionally. Hikers in the winter may see rain in the lower desert, and the monsoon season from July to September may be wet, but the amount of moisture all depends on the overall weather patterns. The weather at higher elevations is typical of mountains: freezing cold in the winter with cool nights and warm days in the summer. Always be prepared for the cold or rain at the higher altitudes regardless of the time of year. Even after these caveats, it is fair to say that, more often than not, the weather in Arizona is perfect.

Hot-Air Balloons

It does not matter how many times people have seen hot-air balloons gliding though the sky, they always have to stop and look whenever they see another. Arizona's clear skies and beautiful weather of fall, winter, and spring attract hordes of balloonists to the Sonoran Desert. It is not uncommon to see five or six hot-air balloons serenely floating on the morning horizon. If you ever see balloons launching from a field, get out of your car and watch how they expand them with a powerful fan, then bring them off the ground with the flame of a loud burner. The flurry of activity stops as soon as the basket lifts. The crowd inevitably stands spellbound as the balloon quietly and effortlessly becomes a speck in the sky.

If liftoff seems exciting, touchdown is even more fun. A balloonist cannot control the direction of the balloon's travel; it is carried wherever the wind blows. Because they cannot stay aloft forever, they are forced to land wherever there is an opening. Do not be surprised if some day a large, orange, pumpkin-shaped hot-air balloon lands in your backyard. Keep an eye open for hot-air balloons. They are fascinating whether they are coming or going.

How to Use This Book

The hikes in this book offer a range of difficulty for all ages, but not necessarily all ages at the same time. Most of the hikes are intended for the whole family; however, there are a few that are not appropriate for small children. Read the information block and complete description for each hike; then, based on the ages and abilities of your children, decide which hikes are best for you. Do not ignore a trail just because it is listed as strenuous. There are always turnaround points that make the hike shorter, and it may also be possible to turn a long hike into an overnight campout so that it is not too hard for little children. In this book, however, all the hikes described are day hikes.

The hikes are grouped geographically into three sections: Northern Arizona, which covers the area north of Flagstaff and Interstate 40; Central Arizona, which covers the area between Phoenix and Flagstaff, and areas just south of Phoenix; and Southern Arizona, which covers the area around Tucson to the Arizona-Mexico border.

The hikes in Northern Arizona range from trails in thick, lush pine forests around Flagstaff to walks along the sheer cliffs of the Grand Canyon and Betatakin Canyon. It can be hot during the summer days, but usually cools off at night. Flagstaff is a quaint city that has all the amenities and necessities.

A hot-air balloon sails quietly through the sky.

Upper and Lower Sonoran life dominates the Central Arizona hikes, which include the fabulous red-rock country around Sedona and Oak Creek. Some hikes are located in Phoenix, which is the largest city in the state. Other hikes are a short drive from the city in beautiul wilderness areas.

With the exception of Mount Lemmon (hikes 31 through 37), the hikes in Southern Arizona represent the desert at its best, including Madera Canyon, an internationally known birding area, and the famous Chiricahua National Monument. The city of Tucson lies at the base of the Santa Catalina Mountains, which encompass the desert sky-island Mount Lemmon, where tall pine forests thrive at the high altitude.

The condensed block of information that precedes each hike is in the following format.

Location: The public land in which the hike takes place is listed here; these include local, state, and national parks; national monuments; and national forests. In the appendix at the back of the book, addresses and phone numbers are given for the various land management agencies that control these public lands.

Difficulty: Each hike is rated easy, moderate, or strenuous. Rating a hike's difficulty is very subjective; what is hard to one hiker may be simple to another. The ratings in this book are based on length, condition of the trail, and vertical change in altitude. Generally, an easy hike is perfect for small children with little help. A moderate hike means the smallest children may need some help on parts of the trail and may not be able to complete the hike. Strenuous hikes are meant for older children who are ready to take on more challenge. Hike 32, Mount Lemmon, Lemmon Rock Lookout, and Wilderness of Rocks Trails, is the most difficult hike, and its successful completion is a major accomplishment that children will not forget.

Distance: The round-trip mileage is given for each hike. If the hike is listed as a loop, it involves very little retracing of the route on the return trip.

Hiking time: The average time required to complete the hike is given. The times are the actual time it took to do the hike, including rest breaks and stops to take photographs. Note that the speed along the trail, in most cases, works out to be about 1 mph, which is a sustainable rate for most children.

Hikable: The best time to do each hike is listed, by month. Hiking during the best time of the year does not guarantee perfect weather, but the weather probably will be good. Call the land management agency (see Appendix) before you leave to see what type of weather to expect, but always go prepared for poor weather just in case.

Elevation gain/loss: The change in elevation is given in feet.

The starting elevation for each hike is listed in the description of the trailhead. The change in elevation does not include every rise and fall in the trail; it is the difference between the minimum and the maximum altitude.

Maps: The maps in this book provide enough detail to allow you to follow the trail, but if you want to know more about the area, the name of the appropriate USGS topographical map is provided. Unfortunately, the only enduring features on the topographical maps are the land formations. Roads, trails, and even the course of streams change over the years, so the trail you want may not appear on the USGS map. Check with the land management agency for more recent maps or brochures. Addresses and phone numbers are provided in the appendix at the back of the book.

After the information block, the first paragraph summarizes the hike, and is followed by driving instructions to the trailhead. Whether there is an entry fee, when known, is mentioned here; for further information, refer to the land management agencies listed in the appendix at the back of the book. Then the trail is described in detail, including points of interest and mileage points along the way. The narrative concludes with return-route information.

Key to Symbols

 Dayhikes. These are hikes that can be completed in a single day. While some trips allow camping, none require it.

 Easy trails. These are smooth, gentle trails that are nearly flat in many places. Small children do not need very much help and first-time hikers will find these trips pleasant.

 Moderate trails. Small children on these trails require some help along the way. Trails can be rough, rocky, and steep in some places. Although the maximum elevation change may not be very much, there can be a lot of walking up and down hills.

 Strenuous trails. These trails are considered difficult because of length or steepness of the terrain. Some strenuous trails can be negotiated by small children with a lot of help from an adult, but some trails are best only for older, more experienced children.

Hikable. The best times of year to hike each trail are indicated by the following symbols: flower—spring; sun—summer; leaf—fall; snowflake—winter.

A Note About Safety

Safety is an important concern in all outdoor activities. No guidebook can alert you to every hazard or anticipate the limitations of every reader. Therefore, the descriptions of roads, trails, routes, and natural features in this book are not representations that a particular place or excursion will be safe for your party. When you follow any of the routes described in this book, you assume responsibility for your own safety. Under normal conditions, such excursions require the usual attention to traffic, road and trail conditions, weather, terrain, the capabilities of your party, and other factors. Because many of the lands in this book are subject to development and/or change of ownership, conditions may have changed since this book was written that make your use of some of these routes unwise. Always check for current conditions, obey posted private property signs, and avoid confrontations with property owners or managers. Keeping informed on current conditions and exercising common sense are the keys to a safe, enjoyable outing.

The Mountaineers

Northern Arizona

The view along Bright Angel Point Trail

1. Bright Angel Point Trail

Location: Grand Canyon National Park, North Rim
Difficulty: Easy
Distance: 1.2-mile loop
Hiking time: 1 hour
Hikable: May-October
Elevation gain: 140 feet
Map: USGS Bright Angel Point

The Grand Canyon is so big that it is difficult to comprehend and even harder to describe, but on the way to unbelievable views, discover dwarfed trees, fossils in Kaibab limestone, and a statue of the famous burro Brighty. Along the narrow ridge that leads to Bright Angel Point, listen to the roar of the wind and feel its buffeting as it sweeps from the bottom of the canyon up over the edge. The paved, smooth trail is an easy trip for children of all ages, with short walls to remind them to stay on the trail. The trail ends at a fenced point where unsurpassed scenery, on an enormous scale, amazes everyone. Portions of the trail are not fenced and it is dangerous to leave the trail. Watch your children carefully.

Driving Instructions: From Flagstaff, take US Highway 89 north. At 112 miles, exit on Alternate 89, which eventually travels west to Jacob Lake. In 51 miles, turn left onto State Highway 67, also known as North Rim Parkway, and drive south 39 miles to the parking lots at the North Rim Visitors Center. The Bright Angel Point Trail starts at a small log display shelter near the parking areas, elevation 8,240 feet. An entrance fee is required.

Before starting down the asphalt path, stop behind the wooden building to look over a stone wall at the deep gorge called Roaring Springs Canyon. When the wind is just right, you can hear the spring flowing deep down inside the canyon. As you make your way along the trail, watch for juniper with its rough bark, gambel oak, and clumps of grass, but most importantly note the height and proximity of the pine trees. An opening between the trees, at 0.1 mile, reveals a distant mesa with a crown of green plants followed by alternating layers of white limestone and red shale that descend into the depths. Look at the pinecones and needles on the ground. Watch for chipmunks busy at work and listen for gentle breezes in the trees. Everything feels like a normal, typical forest.

At the intersection at 0.15 mile, stay to the left; here and at the rest area 100 feet later, the immense canyon comes into full view. In the short distance from the log shelter to the rest stop, the terrain transforms from a common forest to the incredible. The canyon is astonishing, nothing short of breathtaking, and evokes a single thought: how did something so tremendous come to exist? Explain to the children that the Colorado River far below carved this extraordinary canyon over an enormous length of time.

As you come out of your reverie, take another look around, but this time do not look into the distance or the depths; rather, look at the trees and plants at hand. Notice that the tall pines are behind you, and everything in front of you is stunted and gnarled by the hot winds that roar from the bottom of the canyon up over the plants along the edges. Their diminutive size is a result of the pounding, hot winds produced in the canyon.

Descend the hill, staying left at the next intersection, and walk onto the ridge that leads to Bright Angel Point. The trail is flanked by limestone, which is the solidified remains of ancient shelled animals. Ask the children to imagine the billions of crustaceans it took to deposit such thick layers of limestone over such a wide area. Mixed in the dull white stone are shining minerals and round fossils shaped like miniature vertebrae. Together, search the limestone along the entire path to find what might be an ancient fossil.

Both sides of the narrow ridge are easily seen from the small bridge at 0.3 mile, and the force of the buffeting wind is clearly felt if it is blowing. Just before the bridge, a small pine grows directly from solid rock as a testament to tenacity and perseverance. Can the children imagine what it would be like to grow in such a place? Just beyond the second small bridge, search the limestone wall not only for fossils, but also for a drill hole that was probably left when the trail was made.

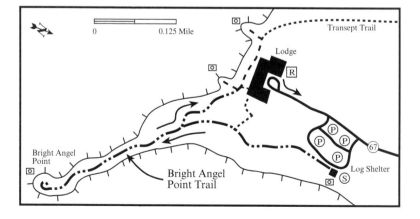

Sunrise silhouettes a dead tree

Bright Angel Point, at 0.45 mile, provides stunning views on all sides and also straight down, deep into the Grand Canyon. Can the children see the Colorado River far below? There is also a log bench to sit on and enjoy the serenity if, by the rare chance, you have the popular point to yourself. When the children are ready, return along the path to see new, spectacular views that were behind you during the trip out.

At the first intersection on the return trip, at 0.7 mile, the righthand path leads uphill to return to the parking lot along the trail you came in on. But stay to the left (on the trail to the lodge); 0.1

mile later, a spur trail takes off to the left to a viewpoint that offers a different perspective of the astounding surroundings.

At the next intersection, just 400 feet past the overlook, continue straight toward stone stairs that climb to a large, castle-like observation room in the lower reaches of the lodge. From the stone stairs, go behind the lodge, past the metal stairs that climb to the right, to the 0.95-mile point, where another spur trail to a viewpoint exits to the left. The sharp ridges, temple-like tops of mesas, and swaths of red and white rock are all on such a large scale.

From this last lookout, turn right onto the trail, climb the metal stairs, and walk across the outdoor patio to the main observation room inside the lodge. This higher vantage point provides glimpses of other parts of the canyon and demonstrates that just a small fraction is visible from the three overlooks visited during the hike. In the corner by the stairs to the front of the room sits a 3-foot bronze statue of the famous burro Brighty, a resident of the area from earlier days. Brighty was first found by a prospector who trained the animal to carry mining equipment. After the prospector died, Brighty once more roamed free and became well known by the people who frequented the Grand Canyon.

Exit the front of the lodge and stay to the right on the road that leads back to the parking lot.

2. Cape Royal Trail

Location:	Grand Canyon National Park, North Rim
Difficulty:	Easy
Distance:	1.1 miles round trip
Hiking time:	1 hour
Hikable:	May-October
Elevation gain:	60 feet
Map:	USGS Cape Royal

A meandering, wheelchair-accessible asphalt trail leads through Upper Sonoran pinyon pine, Utah juniper, and sagebrush to a view of the Colorado River, which carved the entire Grand Canyon. The expansive views of Angels Window and colored, distant buttes are a backdrop to fern bushes with their delicate leaves, holes drilled into the rough juniper bark by sapsuckers, and trees miraculously growing out of

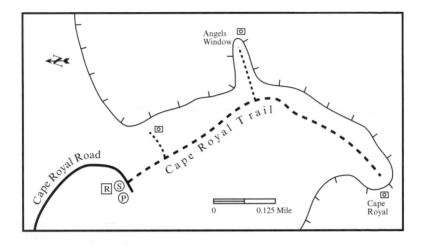

solid stone. The overlook above Angels Window is a cliff with sheer 200- to 300-foot drops that would be scary if not for the fence. Log benches and a flat trail provide an easy hike for all ages. There is little shade to provide comfort on hot days and there is no water, so take all that is needed. The distance from the trailhead directly to the overlook at Cape Royal is a short 0.3-mile walk on a nearly level trail, but be sure to explore every side trail to see wonderful views even though it lengthens the hike by 0.5 mile.

Driving Instructions: From Flagstaff, take US Highway 89 north 112 miles to Alternate 89, which leads west 51 miles to Jacob Lake. From Jacob Lake, follow State Highway 67 south 36 miles to the intersection with Cape Royal Road. Turn left and follow Cape Royal Road 17 miles to the parking area at its terminus. The trailhead lies to the left as you enter the parking lot, elevation 7,760 feet. There is an entrance fee.

Desert vegetation like juniper, sagebrush, cliff rose, and the tough, drought-resistant pinyon pine dominate the plant types along the trail, evidence that the Grand Canyon can be hot and forbidding. A small turnout with wooden benches, only 250 feet from the trailhead, offers a nice view of Angels Window: a large, rectangular hole in an even larger limestone ridge. In the canyon below, thin ridges connect temples atop buttes, and the colored bands of red and white rock cascade from the tops of jagged mountains to the very bottom of the canyon where the muddy Colorado River continues to carve its way through solid stone. The river can be seen through Angels Window even from the first viewpoint. This viewpoint is not fenced, so keep your children away from the edge and enjoy the sights from some benches that provide superb views at a safe distance from the edge of the cliff.

A lone man ponders the imponderable: the Grand Canyon.

Look for the muddy Colorado River through Angel's Window.

A sign at 0.1 mile ponders the number of pinyon nuts that fall to the ground before a tree takes root in the rough, stony terrain, but the other question that might be asked is how the tree behind the sign is still alive. Have the children take a close look at the fallen tree near the sign; part of its roots are sticking in the air and yet its branches are still green and growing. The exposed roots still clutch a large rock that was not enough of an anchor to keep the tree upright.

The turnoff to the left at 0.25 mile leads to the fenced overlook above Angels Window. In the middle of the solid stone overlook, two small trees grow where no topsoil is visible. How did seeds ever germinate in such conditions, and how do they survive, especially under the hot summer sun? The secret to plants growing out of solid stone is a crack or indentation where wind has deposited finer soils and water has collected. The first seed to germinate quickly grows, then dies for lack of nourishment, but its remains improve the soil in the crack, giving the next seed a greater chance of survival. After hundreds, possibly thousands, of years, the microclimate in the crack has developed enough to support long-term plant life.

Along the fenced edges, the sheer cliff of the overlook falls 200 to 300 feet before a ledge blocks the view. Look from the drop-off at other cliffs across the expanse to get a better perspective on the Grand Canyon's enormous depth. The walk from Cape Royal Trail to the point of the Angels Window lookout and back is 0.25 mile.

Once back on the Cape Royal Trail, look for two plants in particular: the fern bush and the juniper. The fern bush is easily identified by its red bark, its fine, tiny leaves that look just like a fern, and white blossoms. Ferns are delicate plants that require shade, but not so the fern bush, which can withstand the searing heat of the Upper Sonoran Desert. The attraction of the juniper is not the plant itself, but the tiny holes made in its bark by a bird called a sapsucker. Similar to a woodpecker, the bird clutches the trunk with its feet and drills holes in the bark to drink the sap. Can the children find any of its holes? Does sap still ooze from them?

At a little over 0.7 mile reach the end of the trail at Cape Royal, where a wide, fenced overlook has endless views of eroded limestone rocks that look like columns and narrow stone ridges dividing deep canyons—all on such a heroic scale that it is hard to comprehend.

From the cape, return about 0.3 mile along the Cape Royal Trail directly to the trailhead.

3. Cliff Spring Trail

Location: Grand Canyon National Park, North Rim
Difficulty: Moderate
Distance: 2 miles round trip
Hiking time: 2 hours
Hikable: May-October
Elevation gain: 310 feet
Maps: USGS Walhalla Plateau, USGS Cape Royal

What starts as a hike through a pine forest turns into an adventure along a deep canyon, sheer cliffs, and limestone overhangs formed as springwater dissolves the stone. The Cliff Spring Trail is an arm of the Grand Canyon where the white and red rock, only seen at a distance in hikes 1 and 2, can be touched. See up close the distinct dividing line between white Toroweap limestone and the thin red layer of stone that sits on top of the buff-colored Coconino sandstone. The thick pines in the narrow canyon and the beds of large thistles under the tall limestone ledges are a stark contrast to the barren, windswept cliffs near the end of the trail. There is even a small Indian ruin along the way.

Driving Instructions: From Flagstaff, take US Highway 89 north 112 miles to Alternate 89, which leads west 51 miles to Jacob Lake. From Jacob Lake, follow State Highway 67 south 36 miles to the intersection with Cape Royal Road. Turn left and follow Cape Royal Road almost 17 miles to the parking turnout on the left side of the road 0.3 mile before it ends at the Cape Royal parking lot (hike 2). A sign across the road from the parking area marks the trailhead, elevation 7,800 feet. There is an entrance fee for the park.

From the start, the trail descends a short slope into a wide, flat stand of ponderosa pines where the lack of thick undergrowth increases the sense of openness. Pine needles and cones lay atop scattered grasses. Red and white rocks line the hard-packed dirt trail. The small Indian ruin, on the right just 400 feet from the trailhead, was built under the cover of a large rock; a sign informs us that it was an Anasazi granary built about 1050 A.D. The word "Anasazi" is a Navajo word meaning "the ancient ones." Little is known about the Anasazi, because they left no written records, but they developed an agrarian society of masonry villages, hand-woven baskets, and pottery with beautiful patterns. These artifacts show they cohered as a people about 750 A.D., prospered for about 600 years, then suddenly disappeared sometime in the 1300s. The cities they abandoned are the fascinating ruins we visit today.

The trail descends, and twice crosses a drainage that becomes

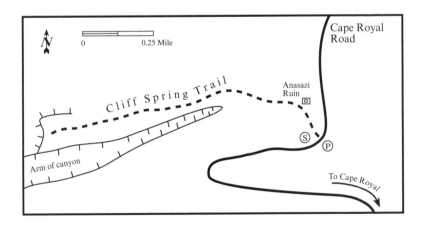

Limestone overhangs

progressively deeper, before rising above the valley and passing between two 5-foot-tall boulders at 0.3 mile. The sandstone wall that
follows rises and slightly overhangs the path. It is fractured, 30 feet
from its starting edge, by a wide, vertical crack filled with a dark
brown stone that seems, in spite of its disparity, to have formed along
with the limestone.

As the trail curves around a corner, an even longer wall with
deeper overhangs stretches endlessly ahead. Flowers grow from the
overhang's ceiling, and by 0.4 mile the drainage along the trail has
become a small canyon whose true depth is revealed by the height
of the tall trees stretching up from its bottom. The sheer limestone
walls across the canyon make the area feel like a miniature version
of the entire Grand Canyon. A short 0.1 mile later, the trail turns
a corner to reveal full-sized temples and buttes. Although they are
at a distance, they are close enough that their large size is made
comprehensible by comparing them to the depth of the small canyon
along the trail.

Water dripping from the limestone overhangs forms pools that
support thick patches of thistles. Help your children to appreciate the
beauty of their royal purple flowers and treat their sharp thorns with
respect. Wildflowers and moss also thrive in the oasis around the
pools. Under one overhang, the springwater gushes from the rock in
its hurry to get to the canyon below. By 0.6 mile, the overhangs end

while the near-level trail provides views of additional formations in the Grand Canyon. Look back to see the tall, green pine trees at the bottom of the narrow part of the canyon where they are protected from the hot sun, then look ahead to see how Upper Sonoran plants replace the pines in the hotter, more open areas.

At 0.7 mile, a pinyon tree takes root on the right side of the trail, grows horizontally across the trail, then turns up to grow skyward on the left side. The trail continues up and down past yucca, pinyon pine, juniper, and small purple flowers until it reaches the side of a tall, white, limestone cliff at 0.85 mile. The children can touch an obviously eroded part of the cliff with their fingers to see how it turns to dust. It is a small reminder that erosion formed the Grand Canyon and it will, eventually, wipe it all away.

The trail turns a corner around the cliff edge, hugs the side, and within 400 feet takes a distinct step down. Look closely at the stone wall near the step, because the rock abruptly and distinctly changes from white limestone on top to a red-colored stone on the bottom. The trail simply ends 0.1 mile later, blocked by a tall cliff with a small window cut into its middle.

Take one last look at the tall temples in the distance, then return along the same path.

The trail hugs the cliff.

4. Sandal Trail

Location: Navajo National Monument
Difficulty: Easy
Distance: 1 mile round trip
Hiking time: 1 hour
Hikable: May-October
Elevation gain: 180 feet
Map: USGS Betatakin Ruin

The easy, asphalt trail leads over red sandstone to an overlook of the Betatakin cliff dwelling ruins in Navajo National Monument. Large stretches of solid stone are dotted with islands of soil that provide root to a pygmy conifer forest. The miniature trees grow with pincushion cacti, yucca, buffaloberry, and other desert plants. Wooden bridges span the natural ditches that carry rainwater to the thick forest at the bottom of the canyon. The cliff dwellings are distant and dwarfed by the huge sandstone arch overhead; take binoculars for a better view. A hogan, another type of desert housing, can be investigated at the outdoor display at the beginning of the trail. Water and bathrooms are in the Visitors Center.

Driving Instructions: From Flagstaff, take US Highway 89 north 65 miles to US Highway 160. Turn right on US Highway 160 and travel northeast 63 miles to State Highway 564. Turn left to

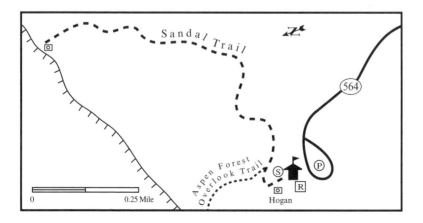

Sweat house display near Visitors Center

travel north 12 miles to the Navajo National Monument park office, elevation 7,280 feet. The trail starts from the patio behind the Visitors Center.

Start the hike at the display opposite the patio, which features a hogan, a sweat house, and a wagon. Children enjoy entering the hogan to see the branch frame that supports the mud exterior, and note the smoke hole in the top. Hogans are still used today as dwellings by some Navajo Indians, and sweat houses are still used in parts of North, Central, and South America.

Just 250 feet from the trailhead, a sign marks the Aspen Forest Overlook Trail, hike 5, to the left. For the Sandal Trail, continue straight on the asphalt path past wide areas of solid, barren stone and patches of plant life that look like soil islands floating on the rock. Ask the children if they can guess how plants can grow on this solid rock. The islands of soil form on a foundation of moss attached to the red sandstone. The mosses' roots intertwine to form a barrier against the rains that would wash loose dirt away. On top of the moss grows all the flora that would normally grow in any forest of the area, except these plants are stunted because the size and depth of their roots is limited by the shallow topsoil. The area is much like an outdoor version of a bonsai garden.

The trail descends gradually on wooden bridges over natural gullies that carry runoff into the canyon. The edges of the steep cliffs that

Terminus of the Sandal Trail overlooking Betatakin Ruins.

form the canyon are visible from the trail, but the bottom is seen only from the overlook at the terminus. Erosion has rounded the red sandstone along the trail, but the circular pattern evident in the rock occurs not by erosion alone, but because of the way the sandstone was formed. Do these erosion patterns remind children of anything? The cliffs are ancient, solidified sand dunes that erode along the swirling patterns of the once-windblown sands. Water erosion of the vertical canyon walls forms round alcoves because of the dune origin of the stone.

Occasional signs along the trail identify yucca, buffaloberry, and cliff fendler, and explain how they were used by the native peoples of Betatakin. The trail ends at 0.5 mile at a fenced overlook on the edge of the cliff. The huge alcove in the opposite canyon wall provided a perfect shelter for cliff dwellings. The mud and stone buildings appear minuscule under the tall arch in the even higher cliff wall, so take binoculars so that children can see the small doors and wooden ladders. The forest of full-size ponderosa pines and quaking aspens in the bottom of the canyon is a drastic contrast to the sparse, pygmy forest above.

A sheltered bench provides rest and shade before you start the easy ascent back to the Visitors Center.

5. Aspen Forest Overlook Trail

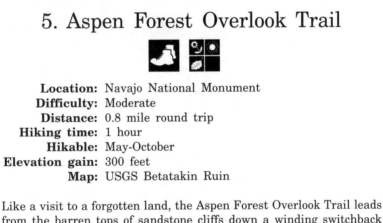

Location: Navajo National Monument
Difficulty: Moderate
Distance: 0.8 mile round trip
Hiking time: 1 hour
Hikable: May-October
Elevation gain: 300 feet
Map: USGS Betatakin Ruin

Like a visit to a forgotten land, the Aspen Forest Overlook Trail leads from the barren tops of sandstone cliffs down a winding switchback to a viewpoint of a lush forest at the bottom of Betatakin Canyon. As the trail descends, the vegetation changes from sparse, drought-resistant plants to tall conifers and quaking aspens, as though nature forgot to tell them that they live in a desert. Plants and rocks crowd

Canyon walls plunge 300 feet from the flat plain.

the trail, making it easy for amateur botanists and geologists to make discoveries. Even though the trail descends 300 feet, a slow ascent on the return trip makes it fun for children of all ages. Handrails along the trail provide support. If at all possible, take the hike in the rain, so you can see the 300-foot waterfalls careening down the canyon

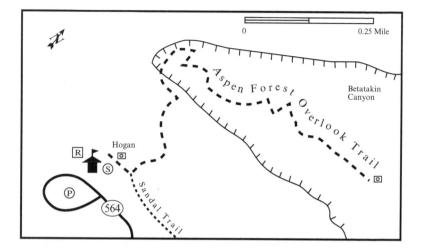

walls. Drinking water and bathrooms are available in the Navajo National Monument Visitors Center.

Driving Instructions: From Flagstaff, take US Highway 89 north 65 miles to US Highway 160, and turn right. Travel northeast 63 miles on US Highway 160 to State Highway 564. Turn left and travel north 12 miles to the Navajo National Monument park office, elevation 7,280 feet. The trail starts from the patio behind the Visitors Center.

From the patio, follow the paved Sandal Trail (hike 4) 250 feet past small stunted trees to the dirt trail turnoff on the left marked by a rock cairn. Even before the Aspen Forest Overlook Trail turns to descend a short flight of stairs, the desert plants, similar to those on the top of the cliff, grow more abundantly. A few more steps and the trail is completely isolated from the world above as it descends into the end of the Betatakin box canyon. Only 0.25 mile down the path, just past a bridge over a natural gully, the plant life changes from pincushion cactus and prickly pear to gambel oak and small fir trees growing at the base of a short cliff. The tops of tall trees from the canyon bottom are visible, but a curtain of green growth, the plants along the trail, blocks a direct view of the entire tree.

At 0.3 mile, just past the second bridge at the top of a flight of stone steps, the 75- to 100-foot-tall Douglas firs come into complete view. The trail continues its descent as it hugs a red sandstone cliff formed by an ancient, solidified sand dune. Erosion exposes the swirling patterns of the once-fluid sand, and etches miniature alcoves in the rock within reach of budding geologists.

Switchbacks twist past wildflowers and red-osier dogwood waiting to be identified by eager botanists until at last, at 0.4 mile, the overlook is reached. The complete picture of the canyon shows pines, aspens, and other deciduous plants only at the closed end of the box canyon, while desert life dominates the rest. The forest is shielded from harsh elements by the high sandstone cliffs. The alcove that houses the Betatakin Ruin cannot be seen from the overlook, but ask the children if they can see the traces of new alcoves slowly forming on the immense, sheer, cliff walls.

Rain adds an exciting dimension to the hike as the water races down the canyon walls and across many parts of the trail. The rhythmic roar and splash of careening water pounding against rocks fills the air. Water from the top of the canyon flows into natural gullies, then careens 300 to 400 feet down the sheer cliff faces to feed the lush plants at the canyon's bottom. A mist rising from the canyon floor makes an already out-of-place forest seem even more wonderful and mysterious. The rains usually perform their magic in late July and all of August, but do not miss the enchanting Aspen Forest Overlook Trail regardless of the weather.

When you've finished exploring Betatakin Canyon, retrace your steps back to the Visitors Center.

6. Betatakin Trail

Location: Navajo National Monument
Difficulty: Moderate
Distance: 5 miles round trip
Hiking time: 5 hours
Hikable: May-October
Elevation gain: 700 feet
Map: USGS Betatakin Ruin

Well-preserved cliff dwelling ruins, pictographs, petroglyphs, stairs cut in stone, loud pinyon jays, and tall mushroom-shaped rocks make the hike to Betatakin Ruin fun and educational. The hike takes you from the barren cliff tops to the lush canyon bottom and finally into the spacious stone alcove that houses the ruins. The trip to the ruins is offered only as a guided tour, and because the well-trained Park Service guides answer your questions, this hike is packed with educational opportunities appropriate for older children. Once in the ruins, look for the original cob of corn in the granary. The hike takes

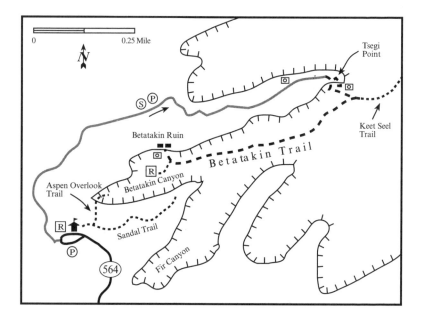

between 4 and 6 hours, with no water along the way, so carry all that is needed.

Driving Instructions: From Flagstaff, take US Highway 89 north 65 miles to US Highway 160. Turn right onto US Highway 160 and travel northeast 63 miles to State Highway 564. Turn left and travel north 12 miles to the Navajo National Monument park office. The hike can only be done as a park ranger–guided tour, and there is only one tour time per day during the summer months; the ruins are closed part of the year. Free tickets for the tour are distributed on a first-come, first-served basis in the Visitors Center, starting at 8:00 A.M., with a limit of twenty-five people per tour. Tour members, led by the ranger, drive from the parking area in front of the Visitors Center onto a dirt road to the trailhead 0.5 mile away.

The first 0.9 mile of the trail follows a wide dirt road that descends slowly over Navajo tribal lands past a collection of box canyons with names like Long and Tsegi. The tops of the cliffs form the flat Colorado Plateau, which stretches as far as the eye can see, while the canyons lie where sheer cliffs cut 600 feet downward. The red-colored terrain supports juniper, pinyon pine, barrel cactus, and other plants that can survive the searing summer heat. Have the children watch for conical piles of sand and dirt near prickly pear cacti, which signal an ant colony that feasts on the cacti's red fruit.

Sandstone boulders near the road display the round and swirling erosion pattern of stone formed from ancient sand dunes. The over-looks of the many canyons reveal the same mesmeric, circular pattern in their large, vertical walls, while some reveal the beginnings of alcoves. Can the children imagine how a people could survive in such harsh conditions? Every tree, each bush, everything in sight had its use in the Betatakin society. The overlook at 0.8 mile displays the conjunction of several canyons and Laguna Creek as it cuts its way through the bottom.

When the road ends at 0.9 mile at Tsegi Point, a foot trail passes through a large groove in the stone to a seemingly endless flight of stairs. These were cut directly in the natural rock by the Civilian Conservation Corps in the 1930s. A small petroglyph is carved into the wall at 1.1 miles, about 8 feet above the stairs, which descend another 0.2 mile before reaching the base of steep cliffs. The now-flat trail passes through juniper and pinyon pine to an intersection at 1.3 miles; the trail to the left goes to Keet Seel,

Original grinding stones

Hikers climbing up to Betatakin Ruins.

another preserved ruin. Stay to the right for the Betatakin Ruin.

At this trail junction, look back toward the base of the stairs to see cliffs shaped like two tall mushrooms. Notice also the mistletoe growing on some of the juniper trees. Mistletoe is a parasitic plant whose roots grow into the branches of its host, and it lives off the host's life-giving sap. The trail slowly descends around tall red cliffs with more nascent alcoves. The large wash at 2.1 miles shows how the topsoil is swept from the canyon bottoms by heavy water flow, leaving only bare rock that cannot support life. Archaeologists believe that the builders of Betatakin Ruin were forced to abandon the city when water removed the topsoil from the canyon bottom and destroyed the possibility of growing crops. Pinyon jays squawk loudly and fly between the trees, but the turkey vultures silently glide from the cliff tops to the depths and back without beating their wings a single time.

From the intersection at 2.3 miles, the soaring Betatakin alcove is visible though the thick trees of the canyon bottom. Bear to the right to climb through trees that hide the ruins. Each step of the ascent reveals more of the alcove: the small doors, the round wooden beams supporting the roofs, and the pole ladders between the different levels. Children enjoy imagining what it might have been like to live in rooms connected by ladders. Green, horizontal lines of plant life around the alcove's interior shows that it formed as water seeped from the top of the cliff, through the porous sandstone, and out the cliff face, carrying rock with it.

The buildings on the left half of the alcove seem, strangely, more complete than those on the right. Later you learn that a stone ledge high in the alcove broke off, obliterating half the village. At 2.5 miles, stand at the base of the ruins, where you learn about the inhabitants' religion, stature, trading habits, and migratory existence. Small steps lead to close looks at the remains on the right half of the village. The entire site, including the grinding stones and corn cobs, is original except for the pole ladders and the carved steps. Notice that some wooden poles have a round hole drilled from one side all the way through to the other. The cores removed from the wood were used by archaeologists to date the ruin. From the back of the alcove, look out over the plush forest of Betatakin Canyon and ask the children to imagine what it would have been like to live there more than 700 years ago. Be sure to see the pictographs painted on the timeless canvas of the exterior of the alcove by a long-dead artist.

Tour members are free to return at their own pace or with the ranger. Going up the innumerable steps by the two giant mushrooms is challenging, so be prepared to make a few rest stops.

7. Lava Flow Nature Trail

Location: Wupatki and Sunset Crater Volcano National
Monument
Difficulty: Easy
Distance: 1-mile loop
Hiking time: 1 hour
Hikable: Year-round (may be closed for short periods
after snowfall)
Elevation gain: 60 feet
Map: USGS Wupatki SW

There was a rumble accompanied by fire and clouds of deadly gas.
Rocks fell from the air, animals ran for their lives, trees burst into
flames. When it was all over, everything laid wasted and smoldering.
Walk through the volcano's destructive path at the base of the 1,000-
foot-tall Sunset Crater. Touch the cinders that cover thousands of
acres, feel the sharp edges of lava long hardened, wonder how the
scattered trees that have grown since the eruption survive in such
a hostile environment. Cinder cones, a miniature volcanic ring, an ice
cave, and the Bonito lava flow make this hike through the strange
volcanic region fascinating. The relatively flat, cinder-paved trail is
a hike for all ages.

Driving Instructions: Take US Highway 89 north from Flagstaff 16 miles to a right turn on Forest Road 545. Follow it about 8
miles to the Sunset Crater turnoff on the right, and take it to the
parking lot at the end. The trailhead, elevation 7,060 feet, is at the
end of the lot.

Viewed from the trailhead, it is hard to believe that the 1,000-
foot-tall Sunset Crater is not solid stone, but instead is a huge pile
of small, loose volcanic particles called cinder. Over 800 square miles
were covered with cinder and thick lava by the volcano between the
years 1164 and 1250 A.D., creating a land of scattered bushes, tall
pines, and strange rock formations to be discovered and explored.

Shortly after you begin the trail, 150 feet from the trailhead,
there is a trail intersection, with the left fork going a short way to
an overlook; take the right fork to a wooden bridge that spans a
hardened river of rough lava. Can the children imagine how the lava
appeared as it oozed out the side of Sunset Crater, burning everything
in its path? Just beyond the bridge, a strange pine tree grows horizontally, parallel to the ground before several branches sprout from

its side to grow upward. Ask the children to look closely at its roots to see that part of them remained planted when the tree fell over, so it continued to grow. Just 200 feet past the tree, the trail passes a wide, flat area completely covered with cinders in which almost no plants are growing. A sign announces that deep under the cinders lie houses buried by the eruption. Fortunately, the slow eruption afforded the inhabitants plenty of time to escape without harm.

The trail winds past sparse plants growing in black cinders until it reaches a fork at 0.1 mile. The right path is a shortcut, so take it if the children are getting tired; but if at all possible, stay left to see everything the area has to offer. Beautiful purple and white flowers along with occasional clumps of grass sprout up through the black soil. At 0.25 mile, look closely at the formations along the trail to see black, red, white, and light brown lava whose bubbly texture looks like sponge cake. Children enjoy touching its rough edges and picking up a small piece to see that it weighs almost nothing. Continue along the nearly flat trail another 350 feet to the entrance of a cold, underground tunnel, called Ice Cave, where the water that seeps through the lava freezes and remains frozen even during the hot summer. Although you can feel cold blasts of air from the tunnel, it is closed to exploration.

A tenth of a mile past the cave is a 6-foot-high, circular lava wall about 18 feet in diameter. Pass through the broken part of the wall to investigate the insides of a miniature volcano. Along the trail, notice that the roots of every tree are partially exposed because they cannot grow deep into the solid lava, but spread wide, just under the surface, to catch any water that might fall. Several trees have fallen because their shallow, wide-flung roots did not provide enough support during

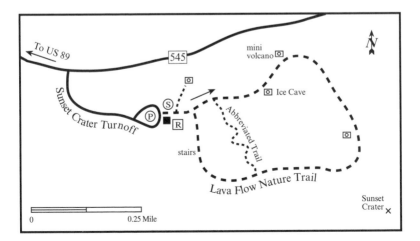

Even after it fell over, this pine tree survived and grew.

storms. The roots of trees that grow in cinders do not spread as much as trees over lava, but instead go straight down; however, the cinders do not offer much support against high winds and several trees lie on their sides, displaying roots that plunged deep but could not withstand the blast of strong winds. Can the children look at the fallen trees to see if their roots spread wide or tried to go deep?

At 0.5 mile, a 100-foot cliff drops to a bed of hardened lava and looks much like a seaside cliff that overlooks black, turbulent waters. The trail descends between Sunset Crater and the end of the cliff into a land of almost no plant life. It is hard to imagine that the hard lava will be rich topsoil in a few centuries. At 0.65 mile, where the abbreviated trail comes in from the right to rejoin the longer loop, continue straight through the intersection. An enormous pine just past the intersection shades a bench where hikers can rest and look at the two different types of lava. Hotter, more fluid lava hardens in slabs of heavy gray stone, whereas the thicker, cooler lava makes the fluffy, coral-like rock.

At 0.75 mile, stairs climb over the lava cliff and past several large lava chunks. Look ahead, along the cliff, to see a lone quaking aspen growing on the edge. Within 150 feet, the trail winds around the strange tree seen at the beginning of the hike, then back over the bridge to the trailhead.

8. Wukoki and Wupatki Ruins

Location: Wupatki and Sunset Crater Volcano National Monument
Difficulty: Easy
Distance: Wukoki, 0.3 mile round trip; Wupatki, 0.7 mile round trip
Hiking time: Wukoki, 0.3 hour; Wupatki, 0.75 hour
Hikable: Year-round (may be closed for short periods after snowfall)
Elevation gain: 100 feet
Map: USGS Wupatki SW

The vast, open areas surrounding the ruins of Wukoki and Wupatki are a contrast to the sheltered environments of ledge and cliff houses. The three-story room of Wukoki is entered through a small door and provides a view of how larger structures were built by early Native Indians. The Wupatki area houses an amphitheater and a ball court in addition to a small hole in the ground known as a blow hole. The trails around both ruins are easy hikes even for young children.

Driving Instructions: From Flagstaff, take US Highway 89 north 16 miles to Forest Road 545. Turn right onto it and drive 20 miles to the turnoff for Wukoki Ruin. Turn right to first visit the Wukoki Ruin. From Wukoki, return to Forest Road 545, turn right, and follow it about 1 mile to the Wupatki Visitors Center parking area on the left.

From the Wukoki Ruin parking lot, notice that fine dust from eroded sandstone colors the earth of the entire area red, while occasional plants provide dashes of green. The hollow opening eroded in the side of a large slab of stone, 200 feet from the trailhead, is large enough for a small child to lie in. Have your children compare the rock's flat top to the interior of the rounded hollow, then touch the fine dust on the ground around the slab to better understand that sand-laden wind carved all the intricate shapes in the solid stone around you.

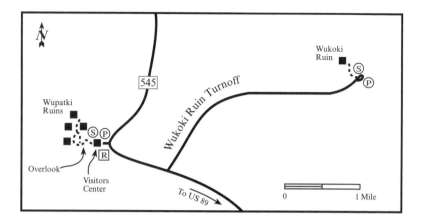

The short cinder trail lined with sandstone rocks leads a short 0.15 mile from the trailhead to a two-story ruin believed to have been three stories tall when it was built. The tall stone building sits atop an outcrop of eroded red sandstone. Compared to houses built under a stone ledge or in an alcove in a cliff, it seems lonely and vulnerable.

Follow the trail to the top of the squat sandstone butte and squeeze through the small door to the interior of the tall ruin. Small windows provided views to the second story, while indentations in the stone probably secured the wood that made the second-story floor. Blue sky shows through the square hole that used to be covered with a roof. The view from the third story must have been impressive.

Look closely at the walls constructed of sandstone held together with mud mortar. The mud suggests that water was available, but outside the rooms, from the flat patio on the butte, have the children survey the area for signs of water. Sparse plant life indicates a dry region now, but in the twelfth century, when the pueblo was occupied, the region was warmer and wetter, providing desirable conditions for farming. Explore the rooms and compare their size to the rooms in modern houses. A short walk around the back of the ruin provides a view of the eroded sandstone butte that serves as the building's foundation. Return to the trailhead, remember the size of this ruin, then drive up the road to Wupatki Ruins.

The trail to Wupatki Ruins starts at the patio behind the Visitors Center. Three hundred feet from the trailhead, the asphalt trail makes a sharp left turn at an overlook that provides a view of the entire site. It is immediately apparent that Wupatki is much bigger than Wukoki, and although the ruins are not as tall, they are more extensive and include an amphitheater and a ball court. The trail widens for an intersection at 0.1 mile, with benches to the left. Take the trail to the right as it descends past multiroom ruins that have not been rebuilt. Entering the ruins at Wupatki is not allowed, so inspecting Wukoki first is a good opportunity to see up close the sandstone with mud mortar construction and small doorways.

At the intersection at the end of the ruins, continue straight to descend to the amphitheater and ball court, which mark Wupatki as being an important settlement. The amphitheater was used for meetings and ceremonies, but archaeologists believe that the gatherings included trading partners and visitors from faraway villages in addition to Wupatki's inhabitants. The exact game played in the ball field is a mystery, but it is believed to be derived from, if not exactly the same as, the game played in Mexico during the same period. Its mere existence proves that the people of Wupatki had contact with other people far away.

Enter the round amphitheater through the opening to discover a stone bench built around its entire circular interior. A fire in the middle would provide the perfect atmosphere to tell stories of adventures. The oblong ball court, downhill from the amphitheater, is enclosed by 6-foot stone walls with openings on each end. On the same level as the ball court, a natural phenomenon called a blow hole exists, but it was not used by the Indians. The hole in the ground provides passage to a subterranean vault of unknown dimensions, formed by an earthquake or by the dissolving of the underlying limestone. High

Wupatki Ruins

external atmospheric pressure causes air to rush into the hole, while low atmospheric pressure forces air out of the hole. Have the children put their face over the hole to see which way the wind is blowing.

On the return climb, go behind the room remains to see how parts of the walls are built right into the large sandstone rocks.

9. Doney Mountain Trail

Location:	Wupatki and Sunset Crater Volcano National Monument
Difficulty:	Moderate
Distance:	1.2 miles round trip
Hiking time:	1 hour
Hikable:	Year-round (may be closed for short periods after snowfall)
Elevation gain:	280 feet
Map:	USGS Wupatki SW

Four small mountains formed entirely of loose cinders rise from the flat ground. The four cinder cones, collectively known as Doney Mountain, formed when molten magma blasted from cracks in the ground, spewing high into the air where it cooled to form particles of varying sizes, then fell back to earth in large piles. The trail to the top of two of the hills winds from the black cinders of the flat ground to the brown cinders of one hill, then back to the red cinders of the other. Budding geologists can compare the colors of each type of cinder and notice the large crack in the Kaibab limestone in the Wupatki plain below. Sparse vegetation of sagebrush, some grasses, and small junipers demonstrates the harshness of the environment, and yet there are ruins of a field house from long-ago farmers.

Driving Instructions: From Flagstaff, take US Highway 89 north 16 miles to Forest Road 545 and turn right onto it. Follow the road 3 miles past the Wupatki Ruins to a sign that says VIEWPOINT AND LUNCH AREA. Turn left onto the road where another sign announces the Doney Picnic Area. Continue to the parking area at the end of the road. The trailhead, elevation 5,360 feet, is at a sign to the left of the outhouses.

From the sign at the trailhead, follow the well-worn trail across endless black cinders sprouting juniper and a spiky shrub called

Mormon tea to an intersection with a bench at 0.1 mile. Notice the occasional light-colored rocks with rounded, smooth edges that are clearly not volcanic and seem very much out of place, until you realize that under the lava and cinder deposited by the eruptions lies a foundation of limestone, sandstone, and sedimentary rock laid by ancient oceans. Take the trail to the left to Little Doney Crater. As the trail ascends, notice how the cinder's color changes from black to brown.

Cinders range in size from minute specks of dust to massive boulders known as bombs, but the rocks that form the cone are not dust-sized, but much larger. Can the children guess why? As cinders fell back to earth, the larger ones fell straight down, close to the source, to form the cone, while the smaller, lighter particles were carried away by the wind. Cones are usually formed from larger chunks, while the light dust is spread over a wide area. A sign at 0.2 mile points out a stack of rocks that formed a field house for early Indian farmers. Many similar rock piles are found throughout the area because the Indians ranged far and wide to grow crops on any available fertile land. Just 100 feet after the sign, a circle of rocks and a bench mark Little Doney Crater's top. Take a moment to rest and look at the pale colors of the Painted Desert and the thin green of Wupatki plain in the distance.

Descend from the top of Little Doney to the intersection with the bench, then continue straight to ascend Big Doney Crater. The trail passes another ruin on the right at 0.4 mile. Soil has started to form from the volcanic stone to support juniper, sparse grasses, and wildflowers. Just past the ruin, another sign marks a spot where Ben Doney, a civil war veteran, dug in search of the lost mine of The Padres. The sides and bottom of the pit reveal only cinders; there is no dirt or rock foundation or any type of geologic glue holding them

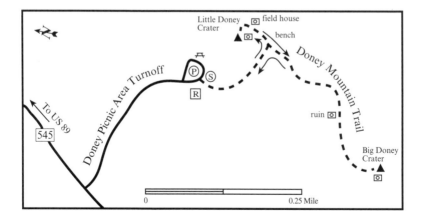

together. The entire mountain really is just a pile of loose volcanic rock, much like an enormous mountain of sand, but the particles are bigger. It is important to stay on the designated trail because each step off the trail and down the side of the cone would leave a footprint and begin to form a groove.

The trail makes a continuous but moderate climb through switchbacks over hard-packed dirt and, in some places, cinders. The climb ends at 0.6 mile at the top of Big Doney Crater, where the surrounding plains are dotted with plants, and a large white crack exposes a streak of limestone in the Wupatki plain below. The larger cone is covered with red cinders, tinted by iron oxide during the eruption. Look at San Francisco Mountain in the distance, which also was formed by volcanic action. San Francisco Mountain looks like several separate mountains because there are three separate peaks; however, it was at one time a tall, pointed volcano until nature removed its top, leaving the smaller peaks in its place.

Return along the same path, making a left turn at the intersection with the bench to get back to the trailhead.

10. Lava River Cave

Location:	Coconino National Forest
Difficulty:	Easy
Distance:	1.8 miles round trip
Hiking time:	1.5 hours
Hikable:	April-October
Elevation gain:	120 feet
Map:	USGS Wing Mountain

A lava tube winding under the surface of the earth sounds a lot like Jules Vernes' story *Journey to the Center of the Earth,* and it is every bit as exciting. A gaping hole in the forest floor leads to an underground adventure of volcanic tunnels, loose rocks that click under foot, and brilliant silver- and rust-colored streaks on the walls. The entrance, littered with boulders, descends to a flat, wide floor navigable by children of all ages. The curved walls are reminiscent of a railway tunnel, making it difficult to know if you should listen for the shrill of a train's whistle or the gurgle of Vernes' Hansbach as it flows to the center of the earth. Flashlights are required for each hiker; helmets are optional but highly

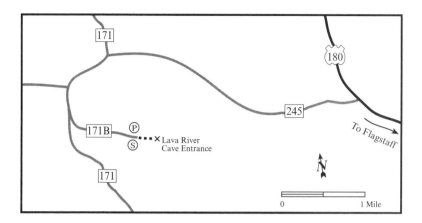

recommended. The tunnel is chilly, so take a sweater too. Young hikers will need help over the large rocks at the entrance.

Driving Instructions: From Flagstaff, take US Highway 180 northwest to mile marker 230. Turn left onto unpaved Forest Road 245 and drive approximately 3 miles to a ⊤ intersection. Turn left onto Forest Road 171, continue about 0.7 mile, then turn left on Forest Road 171B. Follow 171B to the parking area at its terminus, elevation 7,620 feet. A gate blocks the short road that leads to the lava tube entrance.

Follow the road 0.15 mile to a circular, 4-foot-high wall of stacked lava rocks that surrounds a dark hole. Pass through the opening in the wall to begin the steep but short descent, past and over large lava boulders, to the first cavern 200 feet into the tunnel. Enough light filters into the first cavern to see a floor strewn with broken rocks under a rough, arching ceiling. The light from the opening fails after only a few more steps into the tunnel, but your flashlight reveals broad silver streaks on the dark rock of the ceiling and walls. A closer look reveals myriad closely and uniformly spaced individual water droplets that glisten like silver jewels in the light. After a short section of 5-foot-high ceilings, the tunnel opens up at 0.25 mile to the nearly semicircular shape of a railway tunnel that curves through underground darkness.

Flat rock slabs that have fallen from the ceiling cover the tunnel floor unevenly. Most of the rocks do not lie perfectly flat and, like teeter-totters, move as weight is put on one end and return to its resting position when the weight is removed. As the children walk across the rocks, it causes them to teeter, and with each motion each rock bumps against its neighbor, emitting loud clicks like horses' hooves on cobblestone.

The wide, tall winding tunnel continues to where it splits, at 0.45 mile, bringing with it a moment of decision much like the one that faced Professor Hardwick in the book *Journey to the Center of the Earth*. Which tunnel leads to the end? The professor simply followed the small stream of water called the Hansbach and, although the tunnel floor here is wet, there is no such guide in this tunnel. Fortunately, the decision is not difficult. The two tunnels merge back together 250 feet after they split and continue as a single tunnel all the way to the end. The left tunnel is tall and wide, while the right tunnel is only 3 feet tall in some sections.

Take the right tunnel to see it decrease in height from 20 to 10 then finally to 3 feet just before the other tunnel appears on the left. Stay to the right after the junction and prepare to duck a few times through a short section with a 6-foot ceiling. By 0.5 mile, the tunnel, once more tall and wide, displays rust-red streaks on the walls. Can the children guess what caused this? Water has deposited iron oxide as it seeps down from the forest floor above. Notice that the floor is clear of fallen rock, leaving a long 3-inch-wide, 2-foot-deep crack exposed for inspection by budding spelunkers.

Several other short sections have 5-foot ceilings, but the floor is flat and mostly free of obstacles, so passage is easy. Deeper in the tunnel, the air is warmer, with less moisture, so there are fewer silver bands of water droplets on the walls. The tunnel continues past occasional piles of boulders that have flaked off from the ceiling, until the tunnel suddenly ends at 0.9 mile.

On the return trip, take the right fork where the tunnel splits to see the other side. At the cave entrance, follow the road back to the parking area.

---

11. Viet Springs Trail

Location:	Lamar Haines Memorial Wildlife Area
Difficulty:	Easy
Distance:	1.8-mile loop
Hiking time:	1.5 hours
Hikable:	April-October
Elevation gain:	80 feet
Map:	USGS Humphreys Peak

Paradise truly describes the peaceful meadows, stands of quaking aspens, lush grasses, and towering pines of the Lamar Haines Memorial Wildlife

Area. Singing birds and wildflowers along the easy trail make the hike to Viet Springs a pleasure for children of all ages. Volcanic rocks, an old cabin, a spring, and a sitting tree also await discovery by the explorer and historian.

Driving Instructions: Travel northwest out of Flagstaff on US Highway 180 9 miles, turn right on Snow Bowl Road, and continue to the 4.5-mile point; small brown signs with white lettering along the side of the road mark the distance. The sign at the 4.5-mile turnoff marks a dirt road that is blocked by a gate, which has a sign identifying the area as the Lamar Haines Memorial Wildlife Area. Park in the area in front of the gate, elevation 8,540 feet.

Just inside the gate, turn right and climb a small hill to a well-defined unpaved road. Turn right and follow the road past large volcanic boulders and dead trees moldering on the ground. A few quaking aspens grow among the plentiful, tall pines that shade the trail. Squirrels gather food on the ground, then hurriedly run up the closest tree at the sound of feet. Ask the children if they can walk quietly enough to see if the squirrels will stay around. The area was once the 160-acre homestead of Ludwig Viet in 1892. Even today, with civilization burgeoning close by, the area is quiet and secluded. Can the children imagine how it was more than 100 years ago as a remote outpost from the small town of Flagstaff?

Remains of an early settler's cabin

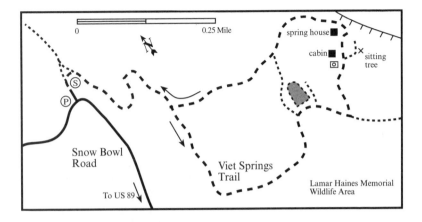

The road takes a 270-degree left turn at 0.1 mile and begins a mild descent down a hill through more quaking aspen. At 0.15 mile, a large, interesting boulder rises to the left of the trail. Its rounded appearance, divided into three sections, makes it look like a volcanic version of a snowman. At the top, a small pine tree juts from the stone like a locket of hair. The descent continues past beautiful purple flowers and scattered boulders into a beautiful meadow thick with the white trunks and delicate green leaves of quaking aspens, at 0.25 mile. Thick, green grasses and bracken spread underneath while birds sing overhead. Have the children look carefully at the quaky leaves. On a still day, not so much as a single leaf will move, but it is difficult for even the slightest breeze to go undetected. The area is so peaceful and your seclusion so complete that you lose connection with space and time. Your journey could just as well be a wagon trip back from town in the late nineteenth century.

A small trail peels off the road at 0.3 mile; this is the return leg of the loop. For now, stay straight and continue on the road past increasingly thicker stands of quaking aspens, golden leaves on the ground from previous seasons, and grass. As the road meanders, it also rises above the meadow and pines are seen more frequently. At 0.5 mile, the roots of a big, long-dead tree surround a 3-foot boulder. Big pinecones, some up to 6 inches long, lie scattered on the ground. Alternating patches of pines and quaking aspen accompany the trail to an earthen dam, built to catch spring waters, at 0.8 mile. Trails cut past each side of the dam, but stay on the well-worn road to an intersection at 0.85 mile, where a closed gate blocks the direct path, but the open road cuts to the left and parallels a fence.

At another fork at 1 mile, the right-hand path leads to a plaque memorializing Lamar Haines and the left-hand path leads to a small,

Quaking aspens grow among massive boulders.

quaint cabin. Without going in, notice that the cabin is so short that most people could not stand up straight in it without bumping their heads. Across from the cabin, the curve in a pine's trunk makes the tree look like it is sitting on a rock. Beyond the cabin, a stone building either houses a spring or acts as a reservoir to the spring in the cliffs just 200 feet away. The stones of the building are natural, uncut and put together with concrete. A wooden door, cemented into the cliff at 1.1 miles, not only protected the spring, but shows the original settler's concern about conserving water. The cliffs rise 70 to 100 feet in a long escarpment of large volcanic boulders, but the growth of trees in front and on top hide it from view at a distance.

Follow the trail between the cliffs and the stone building. Two intersections follow in quick succession; at both take the left fork, which leads away from the escarpment. The trail continues to an open area where, at 1.2 miles and another intersection, the left fork leads to the dam and the right continues through the forest and eventually back to the original road. Follow the right fork as it leads past two dead, fallen trees, one straight across the trail and the other at an angle, which at one time blocked the trail. Trees shade the narrow path, the undergrowth is thick, and mushrooms grow along the rotting remains of trees. The trail for a short time parallels a powerline in a relatively open area until, at 1.35 miles, it plunges once again into thick, peaceful forest. At 1.5 miles the trail meets the road. Turn right onto the road and follow it past now-familiar objects and the quiet meadow back to the trailhead.

12. Red Butte Trail

Location: Kaibab National Forest
Difficulty: Moderate
Distance: 3 miles round trip
Hiking time: 2.5 hours
Hikable: May-December
Elevation gain: 866 feet
Map: USGS Red Butte

There is little difference between hiking to the top of the world and the top of Red Butte—not because it is an overly difficult trail, but

Red Butte rises high above a flat, endless plain.

because once on top, you can see forever. As a bonus, the view from the fire tower is even better. The trip to the top travels through juniper, yucca, scatter grasses, and wildflowers past layers of red sandstone, white limestone, conglomerates of sedimentary rock, and finally the volcanic cap that preserved the butte while everything around it was eroded away.

Driving Instructions: From Flagstaff, take US Highway 180 northwest 31 miles to its intersection with State Highway 64 near the town of Valle. Take Highway 64 north, toward the Grand Canyon, to Forest Road 320, which intersects the highway at mile marker 224. Turn right onto Forest Road 320 and travel 2 miles to Forest Road 340, where you turn left, then right at the intersection with Forest Road 340A. The road ends at the trailhead, elevation 6,460 feet.

A sign at the trailhead describes the three layers of stone that form the butte. The entire formation rests on a foundation of Kaibab limestone, the same limestone that is seen in the upper elevations of the Grand Canyon. The butte's first layer is Moenkopi sandstone and siltstone deposited by water at the beginning of the Mesozoic era. Shinarump conglomerate, small stones cemented together, form the next layer up, while the top is a splotch of basalt, a volcanic rock, from a nearby volcano.

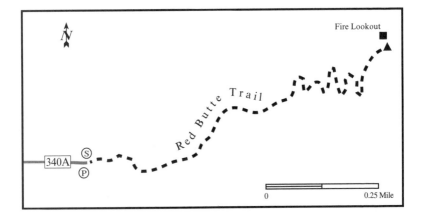

The wide, well-defined trail begins in a sparse forest of juniper and some pinyon pine. Clumps of grass occasionally push their way up through the small stones that cover the ground. The ascent to the top of Red Butte is nearly continuous, with few downgrades; however, the trail's difficulty is mitigated by switchbacks. The sparse vegetation provides no interference to clear views of the vast, surrounding plain, and each step upward provides a better vantage point.

The rocks along the trail tell the geologic story. The gray, slate-like volcanic rock seen along the entire trail has broken from the protective cap and fallen onto the lower slopes. Solid Moenkopi sandstone appears underfoot at 0.4 mile, next to a 2-foot-wide, 3-foot-long sandstone boulder. Orange and green lichens grow on the rocks that cover the ground, but have the children take a close look because they are the bushy, longer variety. There is also a pink material covering some of the rocks, as though they were dipped in something and then left to dry.

At 0.85 mile, the trail makes one of its rare and short descents as the soil changes from a brown to a red hue. An opening in the trees provides a distant view of the reds and whites that color the North Rim of the Grand Canyon. Tell the children to look carefully for a low-profile, dark moss growing on rocks. It looks like mold, especially when it has white spores on top. Children can also touch the leaves of the mountain holly to feel its sharp, pointed edges.

By 1.1 miles, the trail has climbed from the small side hill to the main butte. The tall, red sandstone layer, easily seen from the highway, is now visible up close. Have your children touch the formidably sharp tip of a broad-leaf yucca, and count the joints in a single branch of Mormon tea. Watch also for the clumps of rounded, Shinarump stones held together by geologic glue. Look at the rounded, wind-shaped edges of the sandstone as it comes closer into view with every turn of the trail.

The switchbacks ascend to the level of green-colored rocks by 1.4 miles. Only if they look closely will children notice that the rock is volcanic with a covering of lichens. The trail quickly passes through the layer of volcanic stone to reveal a small plateau of rich brown volcanic rock, cholla, prickly pear cactus, and a few short trees when it reaches the top at 1.5 miles. The view of the wide plain that surrounds the butte is now complete: a 360-degree vista that includes distant mountains and the colored sides of the Grand Canyon.

High on Red Butte

On the far side of the butte stands a lone fire lookout. If it is staffed, you may be invited inside to enjoy an even better vantage point and learn about the Osborn Fire Finder and the special maps used to locate and fight fires. The entire station is powered by gas, so have the children look at the lanterns hung on the walls and ask how the refrigerator works. The only electricity is provided by a small array of solar cells positioned on the roof and is used to power the radio. What do the children think it would be like to live in such a remote but beautiful location in isolation for six months of the year?

Return down the pleasant descent back to the trailhead.

13. Red Mountain Trail

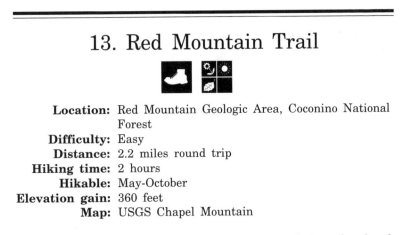

Location: Red Mountain Geologic Area, Coconino National Forest
Difficulty: Easy
Distance: 2.2 miles round trip
Hiking time: 2 hours
Hikable: May-October
Elevation gain: 360 feet
Map: USGS Chapel Mountain

Like many other volcanoes in the area, lava oozed through a break in the earth's crust to form the steep-sided Red Mountain. Unlike others, Red Mountain formed with a huge crater in its middle as though it were cut in half, leaving its insides exposed. Although the trail starts in common desert surroundings, it soon passes huge trees, large volcanic boulders, two black cinder hills, and a small dam before reaching the strange formations in the volcano's center. Wildflowers and Utah juniper, with its shaggy bark, also frame a picture-perfect view of the San Francisco peaks.

Driving Instructions: From Flagstaff, travel northwest on US Highway 180 33 miles to the forest road at mile marker 247. A sign to the left of the highway announces the Red Mountain Geologic Area. Turn left onto the forest road, which soon crosses a cattle guard and turns to dirt. Drive ahead a short distance to the sign marking the road as 9023V. Continue straight 0.25 mile to where the road passes through a fence. Although there is no sign, this is the trailhead, elevation 6,740 feet. Park outside the fence and continue up the road on foot.

On both sides of the wide road, brown cinders from volcanic eruptions cover the ground. Cinders form when an eruption blows out the frothy, gas-rich magma found at the top of a magma column. The lava hardens in the air and falls back to earth in mounds of individual stones of varying sizes. The trail is marked by white plastic diamonds nailed to the trees, which are spread out with little undergrowth. In spring, have the children watch for tiny 3-inch-tall white wildflowers with blossoms only ¼ inch in diameter. At 0.15 mile the road passes through a shallow ditch where sagebrush grows, but not in abundance. Have the children look for tiny, fuzzy plants growing from the ground and try to find any type of plant life different from the tall junipers. Prickly pear cactus grow along the trail, but there are not very many, so the children can count how many they find.

At the intersection at 0.5 mile, stay straight as the road veers to the left. Some of the mistletoe in the tree has turned yellow and fallen to the ground, leaving eye-catching splashes of color against the dark ground. At 0.55 mile, a juniper and a pine grow twisted together as though they were one plant, and a few steps later a small pine tree lays on its side; the glass on the ground reveals it was knocked over by a vehicle.

Red Mountain has been in view the entire hike. It formed when thick, silicic magma forced its way to the surface. Its consistency allowed the lava to build up as a steep cone instead of flowing away over the ground. Red Mountain did not form as a complete cone but,

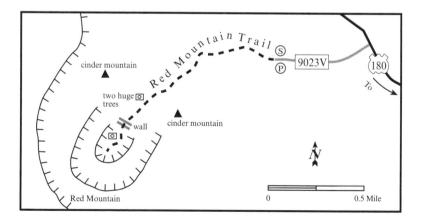

for some reason, as only a partial cone. The red cliffs, seen now only in the distance, are what the other silicic volcanoes in the area look like on the inside.

At 0.7 mile, the road splits to go around two large junipers. Their rough bark peels off in long rope-like strings. A large pile of dirt marks the end of the road at 0.75 mile, and a wash forms to the right of the trail. A short distance later the trail enters the wash and follows it straight ahead toward the looming, red walls. Soon black cinders form mounds on both sides of the trail and signal the entrance into the volcano. Children can touch the cinders and marvel at the enormous piles made of billions of tiny, loose rocks. Two enormous pines grow in the middle of the wash at 0.85 mile, and just a few hundred feet later an 8-foot-high retention wall blocks the way. Tall, pointed rocks with a blackish hue rise on each side of the wall. Climb up the rocks of the wall and continue up the wash.

At 1.1 miles is a tall dead tree. Turn completely around and notice the brown, red, and black spires that surround the inner crater as though a huge chunk of the mountain blew out and disappeared. Children can touch the rough texture of one of the columns and tap it with a small stone. Some spires sound hollow, while others sound like solid rock. Carefully explore the trails around the columns. Notice how erosion has rounded their sides and dulled their pointed ends. Can the children see if birds fly into the large holes in the face of the cliff?

When you are done exploring the crater and its weird formations, return to the dead tree and follow the wash back to the road, and the road back to the trailhead.

14. Sunset Trail

Location: Coconino National Forest
Difficulty: Easy
Distance: 2.4 miles round trip
Hiking time: 2 hours
Hikable: May-September
Elevation gain: 256 feet
Maps: USGS Humphreys Peak, USGS Sunset Crater West, USGS Flagstaff East

Enjoy soaring peaks, a strato volcano, wonderful views, tall spruce

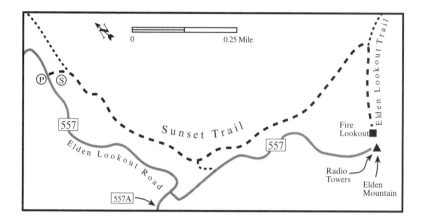

trees, and windblown aspens on the top of Elden Mountain. A short drive up a forest road leads to the dichotomy of side-by-side volcanic and sedimentary rocks, ladybugs, rotting tree stumps, delicate wild-flowers, and the roar of the wind as it rushes to the heights. The fire lookout at the end is a highlight, especially if it is staffed and you are invited up. The road to the trailhead is navigable by passenger car, but it requires slow and careful driving.

Driving Instructions: From Flagstaff, take US Highway 180 northwest 5 miles and turn right onto Schultz Pass Road. Where the road takes a tight curve to the left, go straight onto Elden Lookout Road, also known as Forest Road 557, which is not paved. Travel approximately 6 miles to a pullout on the right side of the road with a sign that says OLDHAM TRAIL #1, BROOKBANK TRAIL #2, BUFFALO PARK. Park and cross the road to the sign for Sunset Trail, elevation 9,040 feet.

Two hundred feet past the trailhead, at the intersection, take the right fork to go toward Elden Lookout. Lots of branches, pine needles, and cones cumber the ground under tall pine trees. Some of the pine-cones are jumbo sized, reaching 6 inches long. The volcanic rocks embedded in the rich topsoil attest to the mountain's origin. The southern half of Elden Mountain was formed when magma flowed out of the ground, while the northern half is a bulge of sedimentary rock forced up by lava under the surface. Outcroppings on the side of the mountain and occasional smooth stones seen along the trail come from the sedimentary layer.

The narrow path winds through trees along a ridge. By 0.2 mile, the tall trees end and a thick grove of aspen grows along the next 200 feet of trail. The blackened tree trunks among the aspen hint of a fire. A denuded expanse opens at 0.3 mile, with charred remains from the large fire that tore through the forest over twenty years ago. A few tall dead trunks stand scattered across the ridge and steep hillsides, while others lie rotting. Small plants sprout from the ground along with abundant grasses, but it is clear that many more years must pass before stately pines will grow once more on the ridge.

The absence of trees provides a view of the wide valley below. Look at the steep sides of the mountain, the outcroppings of rock, and the red color of the valley floor below. At 0.5 mile, all that is left of a once-large pine tree, gutted by fire, is a hollow shell of a stump. Have the children watch for ladybugs in the spring and mushrooms growing wherever the rotting wood is damp. Knots from branches also lay scattered on the ground. Where do the children suppose they come from? As the hardest part of a tree, they survive fire and decay longer than the other parts.

At the intersection at 0.6 mile, take the left fork; the trail makes a short descent and begins to wrap around the peak crowned with numerous radio towers. Notice that the branches of the aspens, at 0.85 mile, all point in the same direction because the blowing winds have trained them. Some tree stumps are not bare wood, but still have a light-colored bark on the outside. Look inside to see the interior wood rotting away, leaving only the circle of bark.

At 1 mile, the trail intersects the Elden Lookout Trail, which climbs up from the foot of the mountain. Go right to follow the Elden Lookout Trail an additional 0.2 mile to the lookout tower. Enjoy the views of Flagstaff, volcanoes, cinder hills, and even Lake Mary along the way. If the fire tower is staffed and you are invited up, you'll see spectacular views from all sides. Look at the map in the tower with the circles around each lookout. Ask for a demonstration of how fires are spotted and located using triangulation between lookouts.

After seeing everything there is to see, return along the same path to the trailhead. On the trip back, especially along the barren ridge, the view of the San Francisco peaks is wonderful. The three peaks—Humphreys, Agassiz, and Fremont—are all part of the same mountain. San Francisco Mountain formed anciently as a strato volcano when thick lava repeatedly poured out of the same vent and formed a tall mountain with steep sides and a pointed top. The resulting mountain would have retained only a single peak, but either a magma chamber collapsed or the top blew off in a terrific explosion, leaving three peaks with a valley in between. Of the three peaks, Humphreys is the highest; it is also the highest point in Arizona at 12,633 feet above sea level.

Central Arizona

Two hikers look closely at rocks along the trail.

15. Island Trail

Location: Walnut Canyon National Monument
Difficulty: Easy
Distance: 1-mile loop
Hiking time: 1 hour
Hikable: Year-round (may be closed for short periods after snowfall)
Elevation gain: 200 feet
Map: USGS Flagstaff East

The deep Walnut Canyon makes the small mountain it surrounds look like an island, which must have given rise to the trail's name. Two hundred and forty steps lead down to the asphalt trail that loops the mountain and leads past broken limestone, tall pine trees, short desert plants, and old Indian ledge houses. Squeeze through the small doors of the ruins to see the blackened ceilings, smell the smoky odor from fires long extinguished, touch the stone used to construct the walls, and find fingerprints from the original builders in the mud mortar. By the end of the trip, see if the children can figure out how ancient inhabitants climbed from the bottom of the deep, twisting canyon to their homes in the ledges of the cliffs. (The answer is found on a plaque somewhere along the trail. Pay attention if you want to know the answer.) Although Island Trail is a hike for children of all ages, smaller hikers may need help on the stairs. Water and bathrooms are in the Visitors Center.

Driving Instructions: From Flagstaff, travel east on Interstate 40 10 miles to the Walnut Canyon Road exit. Travel south on Walnut Canyon Road 4 miles to the parking lot at its terminus. The trail begins at the patio behind the Visitors Center, elevation 6,690 feet.

The patio gives a bird's-eye view of Walnut Canyon as it writhes like a snake across the plateau: The upper limestone layers erode to form the ledges that shelter the Indian ruins, while the lower sandstone layer, left by ancient sand dunes, weathers to look like twisted taffy. From the high patio, the asphalt trail descends to travel completely around a mountain nestled in one of the canyon's curves.

From the very start, plants of all varieties crowd the edges of the trails. Salt brush, mountain mahogany, prickly pear cactus, claret cup cactus, red penstemon wildflowers, and tiny daisies are some of the plants that grow on the sunny southern slopes. The cooler northern slopes boast ponderosa pine and Douglas fir. See if the children can ignore the sun's position and determine north and south by plant variety alone.

The 240 steps start immediately after the patio, pass several benches with nice overlooks, and descend 185 feet to the near-level trail around the mountain. Highly eroded sandstone next to the stairs provides a tactile demonstration of the power of wind and water. Pretty blossoms attract busy bees from unknown places to collect their pollen, and tiny lizards seem to smile as they warm themselves on rough rocks. The stairs end at 0.2 mile in an intersection where a sign points the way to the right. The trail continues to descend slightly under a limestone ledge past gambel oak and ponderosa pine. The plant growth is so thick and close to the trail that it seems crowded and busy.

Ledge houses are visible across the canyon, while the first ruins near the trail are a few incomplete walls under a ledge at 0.25 mile. The larger, completely enclosed rooms at 0.4 mile give a better picture of life in a ledge house. Squeeze through the small door into the dark interior and ask your children to think about how the inhabitants lived. How did they light the interior? How many people lived in each room? Was it cold in the winter? What did they eat?

As the trail curves around the mountain, the tall conifers are slowly replaced by juniper, yucca, and pinyon pine. The 0.5-mile point marks the best preserved and largest ledge houses. Long rows of rooms stretch under ledges, accessed by narrow, short, T-shaped doors crowned with smoke holes. Enter the rooms to smell the age-old smoke residue. Imagine the dim light thrown out by the small fire used for cooking and to provide warmth. Notice the black soot on the ceilings and through the smoke holes above the doors. Examine the mud mortar

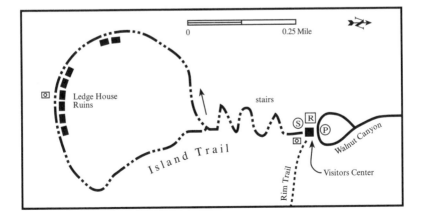

between the wall's limestone rocks for fingerprints left by careful builders whose work has lasted more than eight centuries. All that remains of the house at 0.65 mile is a few walls, but it must have been warm in the winter because it is on the fully exposed south side where only desert plants can survive. Look across to the opposite side of the canyon where, on the north side of the adjacent cliff, tall pines grow. The cliffs provided shelter to both plants and people.

Even on the south side of the mountain, golden penstemons and happy lizards greet passing hikers. The white limestone cliffs that line the trail also offer opportunities to search for embedded fossils from ancient oceans. At 0.8 mile a Utah juniper grows parallel to the ground as though it were a bench to sit on, and another one nearby has had part of its trunk polished by thousands of passing hands.

The stairs begin the return trip to the top just 200 feet past the junipers, and at 1 mile you are back at the top on the patio.

16. Ledges Trail

Location: Dairy Springs Campground
Difficulty: Easy
Distance: 2 miles round trip
Hiking time: 2 hours
Hikable: May-October
Elevation gain: 160 feet
Map: USGS Mormon Lake

A small cliff of volcanic basalt rock terminates the Ledges Trail, but it is preceded by a forest with hidden mushrooms, baby fern bushes, and lizards whose purple bellies are seen only by those who are patient and can move imperceptibly slowly. Pine trees and tall junipers shade the winding trail as it slowly ascends past occasional rock outcroppings to the huge rocks that form the Ledges. Take the time to explore around the rocks and enjoy the view of the plain that forms Mormon Lake. Water and rest rooms are available in the campground at the trailhead during the summer.

Driving Instructions: From Flagstaff, take Lake Mary Road southeast 21 miles. Turn right at the Mormon Lake Road intersection, then turn right onto the gravel road that leads to the Dairy Springs

Just the right size for a first fish, Ledges Trail

Amphitheater. The road is also known as Montezuma Lodge Road. There is a large parking area, 300 feet past the turnoff, in front of the gate of Dairy Springs Campground, elevation 7,180 feet. It is possible to drive through the campground to the trailhead at campsite #25, but there is more parking in the first lot.

From the parking lot at the entrance to Dairy Springs Campground, walk past the gate and follow the road around a wide right turn to an intersection. Take the road to the left through to campsite #25, 0.2 mile from the parking lot, where signs mark the trailhead. The stone-lined, well-defined trail begins in an immaculate, open forest where the path is marked with gray reflective triangles nailed to the trees. In autumn, deer make no effort to flee as hikers admire them from the trail. Some grasses clothe the ground, but almost no dead wood cumbers the forest floor due to the proximity to the campground, making it difficult to find mushrooms.

The first large group of mushrooms grows on dead trees at 0.35 mile. Mushrooms are fungi, so they do not make their own chlorophyll, but live by eating decaying plants. In warm, moist weather, they can double their size in a single day. Have the children look

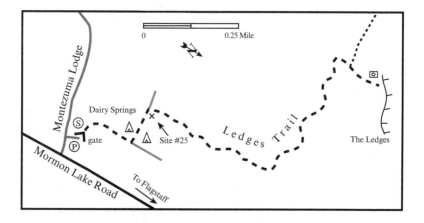

around the trees and in their rotting crevices to find bright yellow, white, and tiny copper-colored mushrooms, and watch closely along the edge of the trail for even more varieties. Look at a mushroom's gills, on the underside of the umbrella-shaped cap, where spores form and are carried by the wind to grow into new mushrooms wherever they land in a moist environment.

By 0.4 mile, small outcroppings of dark, rough boulders begin to appear irregularly and infrequently between the trees. As the trail ascends, junipers grow more abundantly and serve as the foundation to two tree houses next to the trail at 0.5 mile. The grasses of the forest are replaced by flat, gray rocks, which are at times so thick that no earth is visible. The fluorescent orange and green lichens on the rocks provide contrast to the gray skin of resting lizards, but the iridescent blue streaks on the lizards' bellies are seen only by those children who quietly move close enough without scaring them away.

At 0.6 mile, a tall dead tree stands as a sentinel over shorter, live pines and even smaller, 1-inch, baby fern bushes growing at trail's edge. As the trail ascends, the growth under the pines becomes thicker and bushier. Soon, alligator juniper and gambel oak crowd the trail, hiding what lies around each corner until at last a small opening, at 0.7 mile, appears. Wild orange and small daisy flowers push up through the narrow spaces between the closely packed rocks. Trees conceal, but cannot entirely hide, a view of a wide plain in the distance.

Past the opening, the trail begins a mild descent once more through thick junipers until at 0.8 mile it rounds a curve and heads directly toward the open plain. About 200 feet later, the trail forks; the trail to the left goes down a hill, and the main trail goes straight to an obvious plateau. Continue straight the few remaining steps to the edge of a 50-foot-tall ledge formed of the same dark stone seen earlier on the trail.

The cliff is abrupt but not sheer, because it is formed by individual boulders of basalt that look more like big bumps stacked on top of each other than a single, smooth-faced stone plunging down into the forest below. Explore between the boulders at the top and along the length of the ledge to find lichens, wildflowers, and some small bushes growing between the large boulders. Also enjoy the view of the wide, treeless plain that forms the basin for Mormon Lake.

Return by the same path.

17. Devils Bridge

Location: Coconino National Forest
Difficulty: Moderate
Distance: 1.8 miles round trip
Hiking time: 1.75 hours
Hikable: October-April
Elevation gain: 400 feet
Map: USGS Wilson Mountain

The red and white striated mountains of Sedona are the backdrop to Devils Bridge, a natural sandstone bridge. Children love touching the red sandstone that forms the bridge's base and seeing blue sky from behind the arch. The sandstone that can be seen and touched along the trail is a graphic example of how the wind sculpts solid stone. A side trail that leads to views of the forest surrounded by Sedona's famous red-rock mountains invites exploration. Challenge the children to a game to see who is the first to spot the balancing rock on the mountain. The juniper, manzanita, and cypress offer shade occasionally along the trail.

Driving Instructions: From Flagstaff, travel south on US Highway Alternate 89 25 miles to its intersection with State Highway 179. Continue straight on Alternate 89 for 3 miles, to Dry Creek Road. Turn right onto Dry Creek Road and follow it for approximately 1.9 miles to Forest Road 152. Turn right onto the forest road.

The road from this point on is dirt. Follow it for about 1.5 miles to the sign that indicates the Devils Bridge Trailhead on the right. The trailhead is at the end of the small parking lot, elevation 4,600 feet, and is marked by a metal sign that says DEVILS BRIDGE, TRAIL 120.

The trail is wide and well maintained. It winds between a red mountain on the left (north) and a white one on the right (south). Each mountain has colored bands of red and white. The red sandstone was deposited by ancient seas, and the yellow-white Coconino sandstone is from desert sand dunes from long ago. Millions of years ago, the area alternated between inland sea and desert dune, resulting in the red and white bands on the mountains.

At 0.1 mile, the trail turns to the right toward the white mountain, where a large boulder balances on the top. It is visible for much of the hike, so tell young hikers to find it without telling them where to look. Pinyon pine trees and sotol agave dot the landscape. Except

Layered red and white mountains

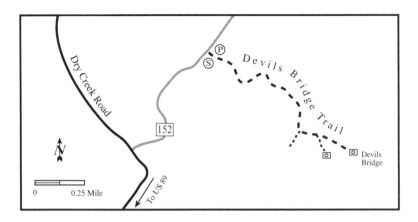

for the green plants, everything else along the trail is red: red rocks, red dirt, and even the branches of the manzanita are red.

The trail is relatively flat until it comes to a wash at 0.4 mile. The trail looks like it may follow the wash to the left, but it really goes to the right up some large, flat stones that look like stairs. Look for the rock cairn at the top. As the trail climbs, it is easier to see the colored bands on the mountains both near and far. At 0.65 mile, the trail narrows and passes a large rock that is black on the top from rain and red on the bottom. A beautiful wash unfolds on the left. Shade lies just ahead under the thick trees where the trail comes to an intersection. Continue to the left on the main trail to Devils Bridge. Just past this intersection, another side trail to the right leads to overviews of the entire valley. The view is worth the effort to hike the small incline. Return to the main trail after enjoying the view.

Past the side trail 0.1 mile, the main trail passes under a over-hang of weathered sandstone that speaks volumes about wind erosion. The curved edges and layers form beautiful patterns that children can touch and enjoy. The trail continues and looks like it dead-ends into a tall wall of black, solid stone, but at the last second it veers to the left around a large pine tree. The sandstone bridge soon comes into view only a few hundred feet ahead. The arch rises from two highly sculpted, red sandstone bases on each side to meet high overhead. It stands in front of a shallow box canyon in the solid cliff, as though nature excavated just enough stone to allow the bridge to form. Hike behind the bridge to get a wonderful view of blue sky and red mountains through the arch.

Return along the same route.

18. Gowan Loop Trail

Location: Tonto Natural Bridge State Park
Difficulty: Strenuous
Distance: 0.5-mile loop
Hiking time: 1.25 hours
Hikable: Year-round
Elevation gain: 183 feet
Map: USGS Buckhead Mesa

Tonto Natural Bridge is the largest known travertine bridge in the world, and the trails getting to it are filled with excitement. The Gowan Loop Trail offers a short section of steep wooden stairs with handrails that descend to the base of the bridge. Rainbows can be seen at the bottom when the sun strikes the water that flows off the top. Pools of water, travertine to touch, and thick moss to inspect are all found under the bridge. The whole unique atmosphere is a result of Pine Creek, limestone deposits, and the natural forces that brought everything together. The water of Pine Creek also supports riparian plants such as oak trees, while the many crevices in the travertine provide homes for innumerable birds. Learning how the bridge formed is just icing on the cake of a fantastic hike. Small children need some help

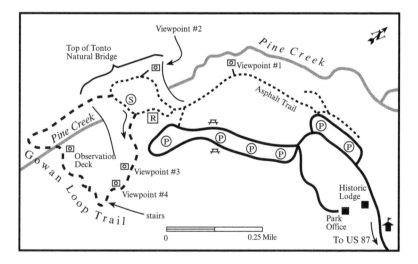

on the stairs. There is a fee to enter the park. Pets are prohibited on the trails and there is no swimming under the bridge.

Driving Instructions: Travel north from Phoenix on State Highway 87 to Payson, 81 miles. Continue on Highway 87 about 10 miles to where signs on the side of the road mark the turnoff on the left to Tonto Natural Bridge State Park. Travel 3 miles from the main highway to the park and, once inside, follow the road to the last parking lot—the one closest to the bridge. A path leads to the bridge and Gowan Loop Trail, elevation 4,533 feet, which starts near an outdoor display that shows how the bridge developed.

From the display, go to the left to start the Gowan Loop Trail. The first stop is Viewpoint #3 at 0.15 mile, where you can see water flowing over the bridge. It was the flow of water that formed the bridge thousands of years ago. Springwater dissolved limestone in the surrounding hills and deposited it as crystalline travertine in the Pine Creek basin. Meanwhile, the water from the creek cut under the travertine to start forming the arch. Years of springwater deposition on the top and creek water cutting through the bottom formed a tunnel 183 feet high, 150 feet wide, and 400 feet long. The water that flows over the bridge continues to deposit travertine, so the bridge is still growing. At the top of the bridge, the travertine looks just like a curtain in a cave because limestone caves are formed in the same way. The bridge from above is spectacular, but it is even better below.

Follow the trail for about 0.1 mile past Schott's yucca, also known as Spanish dagger, around a corner to Viewpoint #4 to the right, and the steep stairs to the left. The stairs are wooden and steep, but there is a handrail for support. Small children need help along the way because the handrail at times is too high for them to reach. The cliff to the right supports red wildflowers frequented by butterflies, while the view to the left is filled with smooth sumac trees that have white blossoms in the spring. Ask children to be extra quiet passing prickly pear cacti, just in case there is a kangaroo rat enjoying a tasty meal.

The stairs descend for 0.1 mile to a wooden observation deck at the base of the bridge. The water from the top of the bridge splatters on the rocks and forms a mist in the air that makes rainbows visible when struck by the sun. Sparrows and larks swoop through the air, then quickly hide in their homes in the travertine crevices.

A gate at the side of the platform leads under the bridge, where there are pools of water, huge chunks of travertine, and large formations covered with a thick moss. It is possible to walk under the bridge, but be careful because travertine and moss are slippery. There is a deep, still pool of water under the center of the bridge. Children should not be left alone to roam under the bridge. Do not try to cross

entirely under the bridge to the other side because the passage is slippery and treacherous, but do enjoy the amazing environment and stunning beauty. Although swimming is prohibited under the bridge, it is allowed downstream.

The trail continues from the observation deck over a wooden bridge that spans Pine Creek. Deep pools of water nourish cypress, pine, and sumac trees along its bed. At 0.3 mile, you reach a short set of stairs that are not as steep as those of the descent. The remainder of the trail is a short, rigorous climb, but the bench at 0.4 mile and the large rock in the shade at 0.45 mile offer places to rest. Notice how quickly the water-loving plants near the creek yield to more hardy desert varieties as the trail climbs beyond the water's life-giving reach. The last few hundred feet of the trail are flat and lead right back to the display.

19. Pine Creek Trail

Location: Tonto Natural Bridge State Park
Difficulty: Strenuous
Distance: 1.2 miles round trip
Hiking time: 2.25 hours
Hikable: Year-round
Elevation gain: 200 feet
Map: USGS Buckhead Mesa

Pine Creek Trail is the second trail that leads under Tonto Natural Bridge, but it is not fair to describe it as merely a hike because it is boulder-hopping at its best. The trip is a lot of work and there are a few places where small children need help over the boulders, but the excitement of finding the best way, walking between towering travertine walls, exploring a small cave, and discovering frogs in the water is worth the effort. The creek flows year-round, but in dry months the bridge is accessible via the creek. Pools of water in the creekbed support lizards and dragonflies, while birds of all types chatter overhead. The best view of a waterfall is also seen from Pine

Gleaming white travertine forms a bridge over Pine Creek.

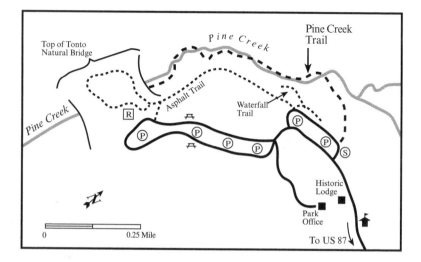

Creek Trail. The trail leads under the bridge and, if the creek is low enough, through to the other side. A fee is charged to enter Tonto Natural Bridge State Park.

Driving Instructions: Travel north from Phoenix on State Highway 87 to Payson, 81 miles. Continue an additional 10 miles north of Payson to where a sign on the side of the road marks the turnoff on the left to Tonto Natural Bridge State Park. Travel 3 miles beyond the main highway to the park and, once inside, turn right into the first parking area. The trailhead for Pine Creek Trail is at the east side of the parking lot and is marked by a sign.

From the trailhead, elevation 4,550 feet, a well-worn dirt trail leads 0.15 mile through a shady grove of Arizona cypress, alligator juniper, and buckthorn bush over a quaint bridge that spans a dry creek down into a sandbar in Pine Creek's bed. Follow the creek to the left to get to Tonto Natural Bridge. The sandbar quickly gives way to large boulders and the real adventure begins. In a few places, small children need help up or down the side of a boulder, but most children find the boulder-hopping so exciting that they want to do it by themselves. On the first part of the trail, stay to the right side for best passage. Watch for small signs with white arrows on a brown background for direction along the entire length of the trail and even under the bridge.

Have the children look for lizards and small brown toads sunning themselves on rocks. Watch as the lizards quickly scurry away at your approach. Large spiderwebs spun between boulders and on tree

Waterfall

branches captivate children. See if they can find the spider and see
if any insects are trapped in the web. Look for dead dragonflies along
the way to get a closer look at their two pairs of wings and compound
eyes. Look into the pools of water among the boulders. Search for
underwater bugs, green mossy water plants, and creatures swimming
around. The creekbed teems with life that depends on the permanent
waters. Ask the children to listen carefully at each pool for the sound
of gurgling water as it runs underground and through hidden chan-
nels behind rocks.

As you move on, the sound of a waterfall becomes stronger until
at 0.35 mile it is visible on the left side of the creek. The water
splashes down the hill, giving life to a forest of ferns while providing
a cool, refreshing atmosphere. At 0.45 mile a tree grows out of the
creekbed and curves over to the bank, inviting children to pass under
it. Two hundred feet later, massive travertine boulders in the middle

of the creek signal the best place to move to the south side of the creek, and the small signs with arrows concur. Go as high up on the bank as possible, climb over the exposed roots of an oak tree, and enter the narrow travertine passage formed by two tall walls of travertine only 12 feet apart. A close look at the travertine reveals fine crystals, grottos, and crevices. Look up to see blue sky between the walls and, toward the end of the passage, note the lone tree growing on top of the wall closest to the creek and stalactites on the cliff side.

At 0.55 mile there is a narrow squeeze between more travertine rocks standing 3.5 feet apart, and just 75 feet later there is a small travertine cave to pass through. The bridge is seen from the cave exit and is just a few boulders away. Follow the arrows as the trail leads down once more into the creekbed, then heads directly for the bridge. Under the bridge, there are huge travertine deposits, a deep pool in the middle, and piles of dead branches that sweep under the bridge during seasons of high waters. Children should not be left unattended under the bridge. Travertine is slippery, especially when wet, and some surfaces are slick and precipitous.

When the creek is low, it is possible to cross completely under the bridge to the other side. Once again, the signs with white arrows show the way, but one section of the trail is smooth and slippery. Do not try to cross through if you feel any apprehension; just enjoy the sound of water as it falls from the top of the bridge way overhead and the refreshing breeze that always seems to blow.

Once you have drunk in the bridge's enormous size and unique construction, return along the same route to the trailhead.

20. Boulder Canyon Trail

Location: Superstition Wilderness
Difficulty: Moderate
Distance: 5 miles round trip
Hiking time: 5 hours
Hikable: October-April
Elevation gain: 600 feet
Map: USGS Mormon Flat Dam

Boulder Canyon Trail provides spectacular views of the Superstition Wilderness and Canyon Lake in addition to rock washes to explore,

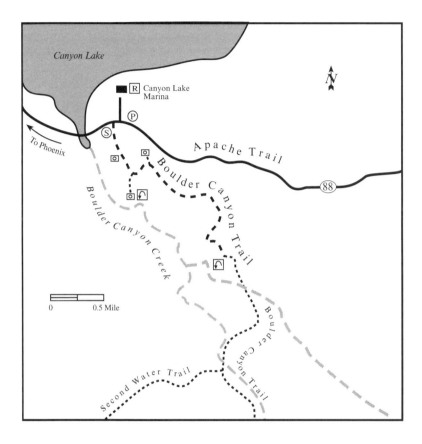

rocks to climb, and birds of prey to watch as they effortlessly soar high above the barren cliffs. The beauty of Weavers Needle, square mesas, and the deep erosion scars of Geronimo Head are the backdrop for wildflowers, cholla, and pincushion cacti. Short side trails offer opportunities to explore, rest, or turn around for a shorter hike. Black volcanic rock is readily available to touch. The trail is popular and you will probably have company. There is no water along the way, so take all you need.

Driving Instructions: From Phoenix take US Highway 60 east to Ironwood Drive. Turn left to travel north on Ironwood to Apache Trail, also known as State Highway 88. Turn right onto Apache Trail and remain on it as it turns to travel northeast 13 miles to the Canyon Lake Marina. The trailhead is on the south side of the highway, but the parking is on the north side at the marina. The entrance to the marina is immediately after the second one-way bridge. There are signs at the front of the lot by the fence that indicate parking for the trailhead. As you walk out of the marina, a sign on the other side of the road, near some white posts, marks the trailhead, elevation 1,680 feet.

As you cross through the white posts, stay to the left as the trail climbs a small hill. The people floating in the small arm of the lake below are fly-fishermen in innertubes trying to catch breakfast. Behind the fishermen rises a light-colored mountain with brown rocks spotted across it. The entire area was born of volcanoes. The dark rock was left by basaltic lava that comes from the earth's mantle. The lighter rock comes from either a thick lava called silicic or from hot volcanic ash that melded together to form tuff. Have the children look closely at the rocks along the trail, comparing the lighter rocks to the darker ones to see if the rocks have detectable crystals. If the rock does not have a crystalline pattern, it is because volcanic rocks, formed from lava, cool too quickly to form large grains.

At 0.35 mile, you arrive at the top of a small hill where you see the sheer canyon cliffs rise out of the waters of Canyon Lake, with Four Peaks in the background. The lake was formed by Mormon Flat dam, when it was built in 1925. The sparkling water is an anomaly in this arid portion of the desert.

The first superb view of Weavers Needle is from an outlook at 0.5 mile where a sign marks the Superstition Wilderness boundary. Continue straight about 200 feet to the lookout where you can rest, see Weavers Needle between two square mesas that jut out of the ground, and touch some dark volcanic rock. A dry riverbed wends its way through the valley far below. Children enjoy looking around the boulders that are scattered about, but part of the lookout is a cliff, so keep them away from the edge. Ask children to search the tops of the mountains and the valley for red-tailed hawks and turkey vultures soaring overhead. The lookout is a good place to turn around if you are hiking with small children.

Return to the sign, where the trail continues up a hill and then doubles back to offer another view of the lake. At 0.75 mile, a side trail to the left leads to an overview of the lake. Look across the water to see part of the dam at the far end. The trail climbs and descends over several small hills, which makes a game of tracking fun. Send a person ahead to hide small objects along the edge of the trail. Make the first ones easy to find, with each one getting successively harder. The tracking game focuses youngsters' attention, so they discover interesting insects, rocks, and animal tracks that would otherwise be missed.

In another 0.25 mile you are on top of an even larger hill where there are overlooks on every side with an even better view of Weavers Needle. Up to this point the trail is wide with solid rock in many

A manmade lake in the desert

places, but it now narrows and plants crowd the edges. It passes behind
some hills that hide the needle and the lake, but new canyons open
to view. Continue up and down small hills for 0.8 mile to a wash of
solid rock that rises on the left. Small depressions formed by wind and
water erosion are abundant. Have children inspect the pockets in the
rock for water, insects, and other life. What do they find and how did
it get there? Some insect life is washed into the pools by flowing
rainwater, while others have hatched from eggs laid by flying insects.

Past the wash, cholla, saguaro, and other typical desert plants
grow freely. Watch for hummingbirds that come to pollinate the cacti
blossoms. Show children that their wings beat so furiously that they
are a blur of motion. Compare the hummingbird's wings to those of

Steep cliffs surround Canyon Lake.

the birds floating on thermals over the desert. A hummingbird has a wingspan of a few inches, compared to some turkey vultures' wingspan of up to 6 feet.

At 2.35 miles, the trail appears to fork, but the right branch is blocked with rocks, so veer to the left and follow the rock cairns. Switchbacks soon begin to descend into the valley. Just beyond a narrow passage of large boulders, one on each side of the trail, the vista opens to the deep valley, revealing mesas and faraway piles of huge boulders. To the east, the yellow, deeply furrowed rock of Geronimo Head rises high into the sky.

The trail continues down into the valley to the dry riverbed, but turn around after enjoying the view and return to the trailhead by the same route. The riverbed is more easily explored from the Second Water Trail, hike 21.

21. Second Water Trail

Location: Superstition Wilderness
Difficulty: Moderate to strenuous
Distance: 6.5 miles round trip
Hiking time: 6 hours
Hikable: October-April
Elevation gain: 480 feet
Map: USGS Goldfield

Incredibly flat is the best way to describe a long section of the Second Water Trail, but not the entire distance. The last part of the trail descends sharply along Second Water Creek down to the dry riverbed at the bottom of Boulder Canyon. In the springtime, water from Second Water Spring nourishes a delightful riparian area that is perfect for exploration or a shady rest break. The wide, flat trail provides a perfect record of animal tracks for discovery and identification. Roam about a field of black volcanic boulders, wonder about the origins of a mysterious, large pit, and puzzle over the purpose of a strange man-made object. Always be on the lookout for the bent saguaro. There is a parking fee at the trailhead.

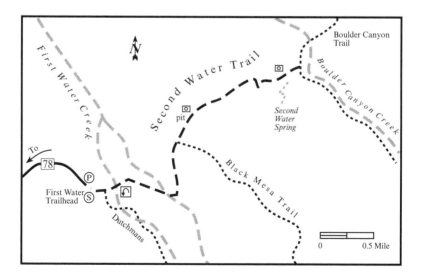

Small hiker sleeps during a hike

Driving Instructions: From Phoenix, take US Highway 60 east to Ironwood Drive. Turn left to travel north on Ironwood to Apache Trail, also known as State Highway 88. Turn right onto Apache Trail, and remain on it as it turns to travel northeast. Drive past Lost Dutchman State Park to mile marker 200, where a sign indicates a right turn onto Forest Road 78 to get to the First Water trailhead. Follow the road about 3.5 miles to the large parking lot at the end. The trailhead is at the far side of the lot, elevation 2,420 feet.

The trailhead provides access to the Second Water Trail and the Dutchmans Trail, which split at the 0.3-mile point. Stay to the left on the Second Water Trail, which soon descends into a heavily eroded wash with large rocks in the bottom. Up to this point, the trail is fairly easy. If little children are getting tired, the wash is a good place to do some exploring and then turn around to go back. The mountains of the area have rocky, barren tops with no plant life visible from the valleys. Saguaro cacti reach for the sky, as does the easily identifiable tip of Weavers Needle as it peeks over the tops of the southeast mountains.

The unidentifiable, man-made object appears just after the wash. It is a slab of concrete with a pipe and two bolts stuck in it, with a piece of wood lying lengthwise off one end. What do the children suppose it is? Part of an old well? A destroyed outhouse? Make everyone guess before you tell them that it is all that remains of the foundation of the old First Water Ranch house.

The well-packed, wide trail continues with slight ascents and descents that curve around hills and plants until it levels off at the intersection with the Black Mesa Trail at about 2 miles. Continue straight ahead on the Second Water Trail rather than turning right onto the Black Mesa Trail; the Second Water Trail becomes as flat as one can imagine. The sandy soil provides a perfect record of passing traffic. At a bare minimum, you will find bird prints, horseshoe marks, sneaker prints, and coyote tracks. Find a spot to smooth the sand, so children can identify fresh prints on the return trip.

Not long after the intersection with the Black Mesa Trail, you will notice thick groups of cholla, thicker than on other sections of the trail. Ask children if they notice anything different about the area. Give them hints to see if they can figure out that the plant life has drastically changed. Once they notice, ask them why there is so much cholla. When the First Water Ranch was in operation, the cows overgrazed the area, killing all the plants. Joints of cholla from other parts of the desert stuck to the cows' bodies and fell off as they grazed in this area. Since there were no other plants to compete with the newly transplanted cholla, their growth took off and resulted in a cholla forest.

The mysterious, large pit appears at 2.3 miles, on the left side of the trail. Have the children guess its origins. Could it be a collapsed volcanic caldera? Did a meteorite strike the earth like at Sunset Crater in northern Arizona? After a few good guesses, tell everyone that it was something associated with the old ranch. The first person to guess a stock watering tank is right. As you continue, be vigilant or you will miss the saguaro that grew up, then down, then up again. The tilde-shaped (~) cactus is just off the right side of the trail before the volcanic boulders.

The wide, flat trail continues for 0.5 mile, then narrows to single file, covered with large, softball-sized rocks. Progress slows as the rocks provide an up-close challenge that requires children's attention. The trail is still rocky, but almost flat. Black boulders on the hill to the left form a band that starts at the top and cuts across the side of the hill until it crosses the trail at 2.8 miles. The boulders vary in diameter from 3 to 5 feet and offer a perfect chance for children to climb and explore. Notice that the rocks are pitch-black in color because they came from volcanoes. From the rocks, look for the birds singing from the branches of nearby bushes. Ask the children to try to find them by the sound of their sweet song alone.

Just past the volcanic rock, the trail makes a very sharp, almost 180-degree turn to the right. From this point on, the trail descends along the stony bed of Second Water Spring to the bottom of Boulder Canyon. The trail is a continuous descent for about 0.2 mile, which becomes a challenging ascent on the return trip. As the trail levels, the sound of running water can be heard in the springtime. The beneficial effects of the water cannot be missed because it has spawned the growth of many large trees, bushes, and reeds in the creekbed. For a short distance along the trail, you are in a riparian wonderland in the middle of a rugged desert. Look into the water for skeeters and mosquito larvae.

A tricky intersection occurs just past the riparian plant life, where the trail appears to cross the creek or follow its bed toward a large boulder. The established trail crosses the creek and, a short 0.1 mile later, it dead-ends at a T intersection with the Boulder Canyon Trail on the edge of the dry riverbed at the bottom of Boulder Canyon. Explore the riverbed and inspect the huge boulders that lie in the middle.

Then return to the trailhead along the same route.

22. Dutchmans–Bluff Spring Trails Loop

Location: Superstition Wilderness
Difficulty: Strenuous
Distance: 9-mile loop
Hiking time: 8 hours
Hikable: October–May
Elevation gain: 800 feet
Map: USGS Weavers Needle

Even though this hike sounds long, it is worth the effort. The 160,000-acre Superstition Wilderness is a collage of captivating volcanic rock

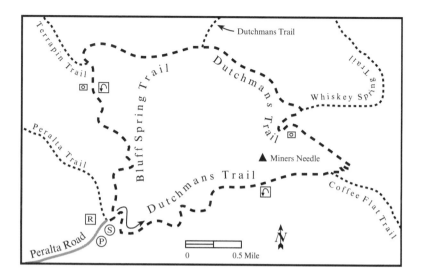

formations, typical desert scenery, seasonal springs, and legends of lost gold. The Superstition Wilderness provides various levels of seclusion. Because it is relatively close to the East Valley, some of the trails can be very busy. Other trails are used so infrequently that they are overgrown and probably frequented by ghosts still searching for gold.

The Dutchmans–Bluff Spring Trails loop carries its travelers through wide-open valleys surrounded by strangely shaped mountains. Turkey vultures hover high overhead while rabbits scurry about in the underbrush. Along the trail, children can explore washes, see two volcanic plugs, discover a window rock, and climb on some funny-shaped boulders while they get their pictures taken. Even though the elevation change is slight, the overall length makes it a hike for older children. If you do not think your children can endure the entire hike, many highlights occur within the first 2 miles of either side of the loop. There is a bathroom at the trailhead, but there is no water. None of the natural springs are reliable, so take all the water you need to drink. The camera should go along too. There is a parking fee at the trailhead.

Driving Instructions: The Dutchmans–Bluff Spring Trails loop is accessed from the popular Peralta Trailhead. From Phoenix, travel east on US Highway 60 past Apache Junction. Stay on Highway 60 as it turns southeast, and go 9 miles to the Peralta Road intersection. Turn left onto Peralta Road and continue an additional 8 miles to the trailhead. There are a few forks, but the direction is well marked with signs. It is a dirt road, but it is well maintained and easily managed by passenger cars. There is plenty of parking, but not all of it is close to the trailhead. The trail starts at the northern end of the last lot, elevation 2,400 feet.

The Superstition Wilderness has more to offer than scenery. The area is well known because of its legends about gold. The best-known story is about Jacob Waltz, a German who is now known as the Lost Dutchman. On his deathbed, he told two friends about a ledge of gold he found while prospecting in the Superstition area. Both of them left everything to search for the gold. One spent his entire life searching, but neither found anything. More than one legend tells of their ghosts still wandering the trails searching for the lost mine.

From the Peralta Trailhead, take the Dutchmans Trail. Within a few hundred feet, the Bluff Spring Trail intersects the Dutchmans Trail. If you do not think you can walk the entire 9-mile loop, take Bluff Spring Trail (to the left) to see the strange rock formations and Weavers Needle; otherwise, take Dutchmans Trail to the right to see Miners Needle. The hike up Bluff Spring Trail is difficult, with loose rock and some steeper parts along the way; the Dutchmans Trail is relatively flat and easy.

The best way to walk the entire loop is counterclockwise, beginning by taking the Dutchmans Trail to the right, because you see

Weaver's Needle

Miners Needle before Weavers Needle. Miners Needle rises about 250 feet from its base. Weavers Needle shoots 550 feet out of the ground and, even though you see it only from a distance, it is spectacular. Seeing Miners Needle first provides a comparison, so that you fully appreciate Weavers Needle.

Just beyond the intersection with Bluff Spring Trail, the Dutchmans Trail gains elevation and then descends into a wide valley. Neither the ascent nor descent are strenuous. The trek through the valley to Miners Needle is flat and easy. Both Miners and Weavers Needles are volcanic plugs that formed when lava hardened in the volcanic tube after an eruption. Erosion wore away everything, leaving the plugs to stand as lone reminders of the volcanoes that gave birth to the entire wilderness. If your children are tired, turn around just as you begin to go past Miners Needle.

Three miles from the trailhead, the Coffee Flat Trail comes in from the right; stay left on the Dutchmans Trail. Just beyond the intersection, the trail turns to the left and climbs around and behind Miners Needle. At about 4 miles, an overlook gives a view of a window rock high on the east side of the needle. A window rock is a stone arch. It is noticeable because you can see blue sky through it.

Past this overlook, there is an unmarked trail intersection where it is not immediately clear which is the right way. Test the budding navigators to see if they can figure out which way to go. The Dutchmans Trail is well worn. Stay on the path that is the best defined, which means you bear to the right, past a small bunch of boulders, and within a few minutes you arrive at the Whiskey Spring Trail intersection, at 4.3 miles. Stay to the left to keep on Dutchmans Trail, which begins to descend. When the trail levels out, there is a wash and several other shady places to eat lunch. The water from the wash has promoted thick forests of paloverde trees and creosote bush. Weavers Needle can also be seen for the first time.

At the intersection with Bluff Spring Trail, at 5.5 miles, bear to the left to switch from the Dutchmans Trail, which continues north, to the Bluff Spring Trail. Look for the trail sign to be sure you are on the Bluff Spring Trail. Notice that the terrain begins to change from desert plants to bare volcanic rock. There are also more and more views of Weavers Needle.

Just south of the intersection with Terrapin Trail, at 6.3 miles, the big boulders off to the right of the trail provide a great backdrop for pictures because Weavers Needle rises sharply in the background. (If you decided to hike only part of this loop and from the trailhead began on Bluff Spring Trail, this viewpoint makes a good turn-around point.) There are parts of the Bluff Spring Trail that are hard to see when it crosses dry creekbeds; however, there are plenty of rock cairns that mark the way. Some of the last parts of the trail are steep, with loose gravel, which makes it moderately difficult.

At the end of the descent, Bluff Springs Trail rejoins Dutchmans Trail at 8.8 miles. Go to the right to complete the short leg back to the trailhead.

23. Lousley Hill Trail

Location: McDowell Mountain Regional Park
Difficulty: Easy
Distance: 1.2-mile loop
Hiking time: 1.5 hours
Hikable: October-May
Elevation gain: 284 feet
Map: USGS Fort McDowell Quad

McDowell Mountain Regional Park has 21,000 acres for hiking, horseback riding, biking, camping, and picnicking. It is a stone's throw from civilization, yet its large size provides solitude. The trail up Lousley Hill passes through a wash that is green with thick vegetation, and rises to a small ridge dominated by cacti and sparse grass. From the top of the ridge, the Verde River can be seen in the distance. The area is recovering from a fire in July 1995; look for the new growth developing along the trail. There are rest rooms near the trailhead. It is a county park, so there is an entrance fee.

Driving Instructions: The park lies west of the Fort McDowell Indian Reservation and north of Mesa. The entrance is on the park's east side. In Phoenix, exit Interstate 17 at Thunderbird Road. Travel east on Thunderbird Road to the Scottsdale Road intersection. Turn right onto Scottsdale Road and travel south 2 miles to Shea Boulevard. Turn left to travel east on Shea Boulevard to Fountain Hills Boulevard, where you turn left and travel north. In the community of Fountain Hills, to the right of the road there is a lake with a fountain that shoots more than 100 feet into the air; everybody is delighted to see it. As Fountain Hills Boulevard turns into McDowell Mountain Road, follow the signs to the park entrance. After paying a nominal entrance fee, stay on McDowell Mountain Park Drive. Turn right on Lousley Drive. The sign for the trailhead is on the right, elevation 1,760 feet, with parking nearby.

Follow the path from the trailhead down to the wash and bear left slightly. The loop part of the trail begins in the wash, where there is a sign with arrows pointing to the right or the left. Take the right fork and hike in a counterclockwise direction. The trail (in either direction) is lined with rocks that must be followed until you have completely crossed the wash. As the trail leaves the wash, the abundant green plants immediately give way to sparse grass and occasional cacti. The trail has an expansive feeling because you are rising over the wide-open desert. Gentle switchbacks slowly lead past clumps of prickly pear, an occasional saguaro, and thorny jumping cholla cacti. Jumping cholla is the nickname for chain fruit cholla because the joints break off so easily when brushed against that they seem to jump off of the plant. Have the children look at the grass. How close are the clumps? Are they green or golden brown from lack of rain? Discuss how plants can give us clues about recent weather.

A bench is located on the steepest part of the trail at the 0.3-mile mark. The area that was burned is still evident. With the children, observe the new, little plants growing next to the blackened remains of those destroyed by the fire. How much has regrown since the fire in July 1995? The path continues with some ups and downs until it reaches a group of small rocks that mark the top of the hill. While resting at the top, point out Weavers Needle, which just barely peeks over a group of small mountains to the southeast. It is a prominent landmark in some of the other hikes. Its origin is explained in hike 22, Dutchmans–Bluff Spring Trails Loop. The Verde River, a rare sight in a desert, is also visible to the east.

The path travels from the top of the hill along a ridge with a small valley to the left, then toward the wash. There are more plants

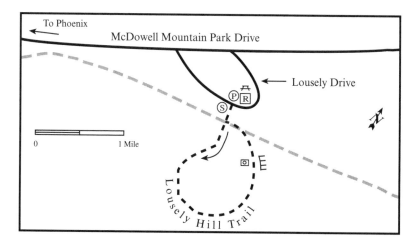

along the ridge than on previous sections of the hill. Have the children carefully touch the spines of the different cacti that grow along the edge of the trail. Even though they look thin and frail, they are stiff and strong because they protect the plant from being eaten; however, some animals, like the javelina, have adapted to eating cacti and rely on them as a food source. Javelinas look like pigs because they have a long snout, but their heads and necks are much larger. They average about 30 inches long and weigh between 40 and 60 pounds. The javelina is a social animal that lives in herds. They eat grass, cacti, shrubs, and acorns.

The next destination is an escarpment at the 0.8-mile point that provides a nice lookout over the wash. A railing keeps children safe from falling over the edge and down the cliff. There is also a bench to rest on. At the railing, play a game of "I Spy" with the children, because the wash has so many plants and birds that everyone will be kept guessing. Challenge children to spot a red cardinal, since even the smallest child can pick out the cardinal's bright red feathers among the green plants. The heat keeps the birds hidden during the day, so the best time to see birds is early in the morning.

The trail leaves the railing, descends through a few easy switchbacks, and arrives once more in the wash. Cross the wash, following the path indicated by the stones, then walk the short distance to the trailhead.

24. Lookout Mountain Circumference Trail

Locations:	Phoenix Mountains Preserve, Lookout Mountain Recreation Area
Difficulty:	Easy; side trip moderate
Distance:	2.6-mile loop; 1.2-mile side trip to summit
Hiking time:	2.5 hours; 1-hour side trip to summit
Hikable:	October-May
Elevation gain:	90 feet; 414 feet on side trip to summit
Maps:	USGS Sunnyslope, USGS Union Hills

Lookout Mountain offers desert solitude in the middle of the city of Phoenix. The Circumference Trail circles the entire park, but there

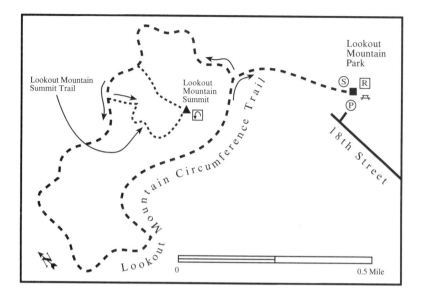

are numerous other trails that cut across the mountain and even go to the top. The optional side trip to the summit can be made on one of two trails. The easy trail to the peak is nice for younger children, while the steep trail makes the older children feel like mountaineers. Rabbits, lizards, and an occasional rock climber provide an unpredictable element to the hike. The trails are marked with brown posts that have trail numbers. The Circumference Trail stays toward the outside part of the park, so it is easy to guess which trail to take even though a marker is not in sight. The park is a preservation area, so do not pick up anything or destroy any vegetation. If your children are too small to walk the entire circumference and climb to the peak, head straight for the peak.

Driving Instructions: The Circumference Trail is easily accessible from Lookout Mountain Park, which is on the south side of the mountain. In Phoenix, from Cave Creek Road, go west on Sharon Drive. In 0.5 mile, turn right onto 18th Street and go north until the street ends at 0.7 mile. The park entrance is on the right. The trailhead is in the northern section of the parking lot, elevation 1,550 feet.

From the trailhead, walk just over 0.25 mile from the bathrooms to where the loop trail begins, then go to the right to hike the loop counterclockwise. At unmarked intersections, always take the lower-altitude trail to stay on the Circumference Trail. Lookout Mountain is on the left as you go around it. The trail is nearly flat and has an open feeling. The brittlebush and creosote bush dotted around the landscape color the park with yellow blossoms in the spring.

There are two types of rabbits common to desert areas: the cottontail and the black-tailed jackrabbit. Cottontails have white tails and are smaller than jackrabbits. At birth, the cottontail young are blind and nearly hairless, and are cared for in a nest until they are weaned at one month. Jackrabbits, much larger than cottontails, have long legs and gigantic ears that make them much easier to see. Baby jackrabbits have fur, can see, and are active at birth. See if the children can spot any rabbits before the animals move. Even in an area of sparse plant life, it is hard to see rabbits because they blend in with the surroundings, but children may detect their ears as a rabbit sits quietly in the shade of a small bush. Reserve a treat for the first child who sees a rabbit before it moves.

As you approach the north side of the mountain, you must decide whether to make the side trip to the summit. The first trail to the top is a steep, wide gravel path that leads directly to the peak. It narrows near the top, with the last 18 feet a vertical climb. Older children can scramble to the top with no problems. For those with younger children, follow the Circumference Trail past the water tank to the Lookout Mountain Summit Trail intersection, at 0.9 mile. To make the side trip to the summit, take the Summit Trail to the left, which is an easy, meandering path. As you climb in altitude, you can clearly see the other mountains in the park just to the right. About halfway up, there are some tall rocks that offer shade and a place to sit. The view from the flat area on top of the mountain reveals the entire park and thousands of houses spread between nearby peaks. The Summit Trail climbs to 2,054 feet. Going to and from the peak adds 1.2 miles and about an hour to the hike. When you've enjoyed the view, hike back down the way you came up.

When you return from the peak, pick up the Circumference Trail where you left off, turning left to continue the loop hike. At the next marked intersection, at 1.4 miles, stay to the right until you begin a short climb to a saddle. Over the saddle, the walk around the westernmost mountain takes you almost into the backyards of some exclusive houses that highlight the purpose of the preserve lands: to provide open space for humans and animals in an otherwise crowded area. Soon the trail turns left around the mountain and heads toward a shallow wash at the 2-mile point. Have the children look closely at the plants near the wash. Usually vegetation near a wash is more abundant, but here the amount of land that drains into the wash is small, so there is not a noticeable increase in the number of plants.

Beyond the wash, a sheer cliff forms the mountain to the left in the distance. It is not unusual to see rock climbers slowly working their way up the cliff; the rope that protects them from a fall is barely visible from the trail's vantage point. Ask the children to look closely along the trail for dark-colored rocks. If a rock shines a little, it may be covered with a thin coat of baked-on dust called desert varnish. Children can also watch for prickly pear cactus, lizards sunning themselves, and the small holes in the ground that mark an ant colony. The beauties of the desert are abundant to the keen eye.

When you arrive back at the start of the loop at 2.35 miles, go to the right for the short leg back to the trailhead.

25. Pass Mountain Trail

Location: Usery Mountain Recreation Area
Difficulty: Moderate
Distance: 7.1-mile loop
Hiking time: 6 hours
Hikable: October-May
Elevation gain: 700 feet
Map: USGS Apache Junction

Take the loop trail around Pass Mountain in March or April to see the Lower Sonoran Life Zone in riotous bloom. All varieties of desert plants can be inspected and touched without leaving the Pass Mountain Trail. The occasional dead saguaro fascinates children. Over a dozen washes must be traversed, and some invite exploring to look at rocks. The hummingbirds buzzing around the cacti and turkey vultures hovering overhead are only part of the area's animal life. Watch for a saguaro cactus that has six arms that bend down and around its body. Travel in a clockwise direction so that the steeper sections, on the east side of the mountain, are descended rather than ascended. Most of the plant life and the best washes occur in the first mile from the trailhead, so the trip can be shortened for little children and you will still see most of the plants. There are bathrooms and water near the trailhead. A nominal fee is charged to enter the park.

Driving Instructions: Usery Mountain Recreation Area is on the east side of Usery Pass Road. In Phoenix, take US Highway 60 east to Ellsworth Road and travel north on Ellsworth Road 7 miles

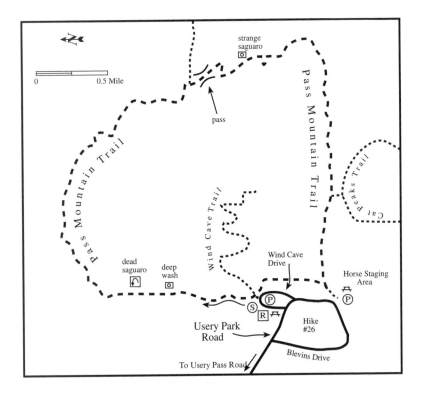

to the park entrance. Above McKellips Road, Ellsworth Road turns into Usery Pass Road; stay on it until you see signs to turn right into the park. Once in the park, take Usery Park Road to the turnoff, on the left, for Wind Cave Drive. Turn left onto Wind Cave Drive and proceed a short distance until you see the bathrooms. There is a lot of convenient parking nearby. The trailhead, elevation 1,900 feet, is to the right and behind the bathrooms.

At the trailhead, Pass Mountain stands directly ahead with a band of yellow rock cutting across its face. The barren rock of the mountain is a contrast to the abundance of desert plants along the trail. A sign shows the Pass Mountain Trail to both the left and the right. Go to the left to travel clockwise around the mountain.

From the beginning of the trail, there are a variety of plants. Have the children look for a round, squat barrel cactus. Notice that it does not grow straight up into the air; it leans noticeably southward because it grows toward the most constant source of sunlight throughout the year. These cacti are also known as the compass cactus because they consistently point in the same direction.

The first of many washes cuts across the trail at 0.15 mile. The trail is hard earth covered with decomposed granite in some places. A deep wash at 0.7 mile has 8-foot-tall rocks lining its sides that protect it from the gouging, erosive force of rainwater. Just beyond the wash, a dead saguaro cactus lies next to the trail. Although the roots of a saguaro spread out as far as the cactus is tall, they do not grow deeply. Shallow roots have the advantage of collecting any scarce rain that may fall, but they cannot provide the support necessary to keep the cactus from blowing over in strong winds. This dead saguaro is a good turnaround point for those hiking with little children.

Point out to children the buckthorn, teddy bear cholla, and chain fruit cholla that grow abundantly next to the trail along with prickly pear cactus and brittlebush. Enjoy the blooms brought to every plant by spring, and listen to the birds. Nourished only by natural rainfall, most desert plants store enough water to bloom even when there is little or no precipitation for as long as a year. Desert reptiles crawl out of their homes to warm in the sun. Lizards are plentiful and usually easy to spot, but count yourself lucky if you see a snake.

As the trail begins to curve around the mountain, a sign at 1.2 miles marks the boundary to the Tonto National Forest. Once around the north end of the mountain, the plant life and terrain change drastically. The saguaro and other cacti decrease in number while scrub bushes like creosote, as well as boulders, dominate the scene. By the 2-mile mark, a large valley opens to the left, with tall mountains in the distance, including Four Peaks. The serenity of the quiet valley is not broken by the silent gliding of vultures overhead. In another 0.4 mile, the trail hugs the mountain on the right as it descends into a gulch that makes a perfect place to rest in the shade.

At about 3 miles, the trail appears to break off to the left to go around some small mountains, but continue straight ahead. Directly in front of the mountains is another good place to rest because they provide some nice shade. Watch for hummingbirds that arrive to drink the flowers' nectar. The creosote bush also displays its yellow blossoms on branches covered in a black tar-like substance. The substance on the branches and the bush's small leaves minimize water loss and enable it to survive drought. The trail begins a steep descent through a pass between two hills just after the trail to the left, and little children may need a helping hand.

The next phenomenal plant is only 0.4 mile ahead. As the trail passes through a wash, have the children watch for a saguaro that has six arms twisting down and around its body—an unusual pose for a cactus. No one really knows why some saguaro arms grow in such strange directions. As the trail continues around the southeast

A small cavern formed by boulders

corner of the mountain, the plants grow closer together and the washes appear with more frequency.

At 5.2 miles, the turnoff to Cat Peaks Trail intersects to the left. One and a half miles later, at the fork in the road where the trail to the left goes to the horse staging area (simply a large dirt parking lot equipped with hitching posts where horse riders can tie their animals while they saddle them), stay on the trail to the right to go back to the trailhead. On the main trail, after several washes and many desert plants, the parking lot appears ahead. You have just completed a hike through a perfect example of the Lower Sonoran Desert.

26. Merkle and Vista Trails

Location: Usery Mountain Recreation Area
Difficulty: Easy
Distance: 1.2 miles round trip
Hiking time: 1.25 hours, plus exploring time
Hikable: October-April
Elevation gain: 118 feet
Map: USGS Apache Junction

The Merkle and Vista Trails are in the Usery Mountain Recreation Area also visited in hike 25, Pass Mountain Trail. The two small mountains crossed by the Vista Trail provide as much fun for older children as they do for the younger ones. The mountains are just high enough to make children feel like they have climbed something without wearing them out; on top there is a jumble of rocks and trail to explore. The Vista Trail ascends one small mountain, descends into a small valley, then climbs to the top of another small mountain. The larger rocks at the saddle between the two mountains are perfect for climbing. Lizards come out from nowhere to catch each child's interest, while black butterflies flutter about. The Merkle Trail loop is a nature trail with signs marking and describing the local plants. Use the signs to learn more about plants that are common to the Lower Sonoran Desert. Even though both trails are short, plan to spend extra time exploring.

Driving Instructions: From Phoenix, take US Highway 60 east to the Ellsworth Road intersection and travel north on Ellsworth Road 7 miles to the park entrance. Above McKellips Road, Ellsworth Road turns into Usery Pass Road; stay on it until you see signs to turn right into the park. Once in the park, continue straight on Usery Park Road to covered picnic shelter #6, just past Wind Cave Drive on the right side of the road. Parking is by the picnic shelter, elevation 1,960 feet.

A short spur trail starts just below the second picnic shelter, where stones mark the path across a wash. There is a large, dead saguaro right in the wash that children can see up close. Once a cactus blows over or dies, the flesh rots away and exposes the stiff cords, which act like a skeleton. The cords do not start growing until the cactus is seven years old, and it takes years for them to decompose after the cactus is dead.

In 0.1 mile reach the Merkle Trail, which goes around the two

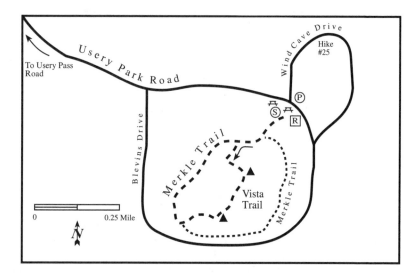

small mountains (the Vista Trail goes over them). Because it is impossible to get lost, you can go in either direction on the Merkle Trail until you find either end of the Vista Trail going up the side of the hill. The hike described here takes the Merkle Trail to the right.

At 0.2 mile, arrive at the Vista Trail junction. Take it to the left and head uphill. The Vista Trail switches back and forth up the hill. The peaks offer a good view of the entire area and the desert plants that grow as far as the eye can see. The trail leads from the first peak to a valley between the small mountains in 0.4 mile, where boulders ranging from 2 to 6 feet tall provide a place to sit and watch for birds, bees, and lizards.

Continue across the saddle to the other peak, and down the Vista Trail to its other end's intersection with the Merkle Trail at 0.6 mile. Go right on the Merkle Trail. Cacti and other plants stand ready for discovery and identification along the Merkle Trail, and many plants are described in trailside signs. Orange and green lichens add splashes of color to the rocks scattered throughout the area. The variety of plants and the twisting trail that rises and falls on the slopes provide unlimited amounts of exploration and fun for all children. Climbing the hills provides a sense of accomplishment without overexertion. If you have enough time, explore the other half of the Merkle Trail.

In another 0.4 mile, reach the intersection of Merkle and Vista Trails where you first ascended via the Vista Trail. Stay left on the Merkle Trail and arrive back at the wash at 1.1 miles; take the short spur trail to the left back to the trailhead at the parking area.

27. Camelback Summit Trail

Location: Echo Canyon Recreation Area
Difficulty: Strenuous
Distance: 2.3 miles round trip
Hiking time: 2.5 hours
Hikable: October-April
Elevation gain: 1,304 feet
Map: USGS Paradise Valley

Energetic is the best word to describe the hike to the top of Camelback Mountain. Certainly you need to be energetic to make it to the top, but there are so many people who zoom to the summit for exercise that you are carried along in the flow of their energy. There is a palpable charge of enthusiasm in the air, but the exuberant people are only a part of the picture. The trail offers indentations in the cliffs that children love to explore, boulders to hop, strangely shaped rocks, and beautiful views of mountain and city, with steep sections of trail that require handrails. Only the first 0.1 mile is meant for little children, while the last mile is for the hardy older ones. There is never a dull moment during the short but strenuous jaunt to the summit.

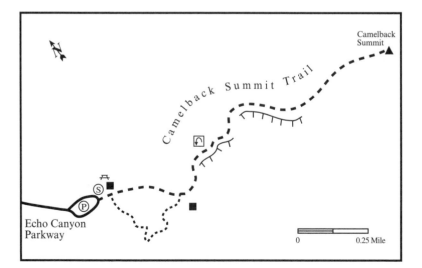

Driving Instructions: Echo Canyon Park lies between Paradise Valley, Scottsdale, and the Phoenix Mountain Preserve. From US Highway 60 in Phoenix, take Rural Road, whose name later changes to Scottsdale Road, north for 11 miles. Turn left at McDonald Drive, then in 3 miles, just before the light at Tatum Boulevard, turn left onto Echo Canyon Parkway. The road dead-ends in the parking lot, elevation 1,400 feet. Camelback is a popular place, so if the small lot is full, you may have to park on the street.

The trail starts at the covered picnic shelter at the east end of the parking lot. Follow the stairs to the left that climb the hill, where squirrels live in the brush. The trail passes a huge boulder covered with chalk marks from practicing rock climbers. If any are there, the children will want to watch how they carefully work their way up the rock face.

Beyond the boulder, there is an intersection at 0.25 mile. Continue straight ahead, where the trail goes between a tall cliff of volcanic tuff on the right and a fence to the left. The face of the cliff is irregular, with indentations and bulges that children can touch from the trail. Ask them to look at the hollows to see if they are smooth from erosion or rough from their day of formation.

At about 0.38 mile (⅜ mile), a handrail assists on a very steep section of the trail; this is the turnaround point for small children. Those with older children should proceed up the hill with care, because the rock around the handrails is slick from so much wear. There are no tedious sections on this hike; children are intensely involved during the entire distance.

A short landing follows a second railing, at 0.5 mile, where you can catch your breath if you can resist the upward flow of energy. Near the trail, more rocks with indentations cut by wind erosion await discovery before you continue the climb. Views of an expansive city are contrasted by the strange rock formations composed of granite, schist, and gravel, which represent the three different classes of rocks: igneous, metamorphic, and sedimentary, respectively. The rest of the trail to the top is not as steep as the first parts, but climbing over numerous boulders offers continuous exertion. Although this is challenging for children, they receive endless compliments and encouragement from fellow hikers along the way.

At 0.63 mile (⅝ mile), the rough cliff still rises to one side while large boulders lie piled in the trail. Notice the branches of the paloverde tree growing in the middle of the trail. They are smooth and polished by the thousands of hands that grab them each year for support.

The trail continues to gain altitude as you climb over rocks until

Moon rising over Echo Canyon

you reach the broad summit at 1.15 miles. The view is beautiful because you can see all the mountains of the Phoenix Mountain Preserve, dense housing, and, further in the distance, a large checkerboard of plowed and planted fields. Swifts fly around the summit, and occasionally a helicopter whisks by at a low altitude.

Return by the same route. When you reach the railings, it is easier to go down backward.

28. North Mountain National Trail

Locations: Phoenix Mountains Preserve, North Mountain Recreation Area
Difficulty: Moderate
Distance: 1.6-mile loop
Hiking time: 2.5 hours
Hikable: October-April
Elevation gain: 614 feet
Map: USGS Sunnyslope

The rise and fall of the terrain give the relatively short National Trail the feel of a much longer expedition. The trail ascends one side of North Mountain, passes outcrops of black, broken volcanic rock, and descends on the other side. It offers steep sections that challenge but do not overwhelm the little hiker. There are rocks to climb on, lots of brittlebush and creosote bush, hard quartz rocks to inspect, and beautiful views of desert and city. Chipmunks and birds are easily spotted along the trail. Before starting the hike, take a 10-minute trip around the Penny Howe Nature Trail to learn the names of desert plants. Bathrooms and water are at the trailhead.

Driving Instructions: From Interstate 10 in Phoenix, go north on Highway 51 9 miles, exit at Northern Avenue, and turn left (west). In 2 miles, turn right onto Seventh Street, then in 2.5 miles turn left at Peoria Avenue into the entrance of the North Mountain Recreation Area. Stay right at the next intersection to travel the road inside the park counterclockwise, and park your vehicle next to the park office. Walk on the road back to the trailhead, elevation 1,490 feet, just behind the Maricopa covered picnic shelter. If you wish to hike the Penny Howe Nature Trail, it is located south of the parking area.

The National Trail begins with a flight of stairs made of natural

Descending North Mountain

stone. A friendly saguaro seems to wave as you pass by it on the stair climb. From the landing at the top of the stairs, veer to the right, avoiding the dirt trail to the left, to get to a paved service road. The road leads, with a mild ascent, past small cliffs on the left. Colorful spring wildflowers cover the ground and burst from any crack in the stone where roots can take hold. Ask the children to look at them closely. How many different colors can they find? How many petals emerge from a single blossom? Watch for the small, violet blossom of desert lavender because it blooms year-round.

Near the end of the paved road at 0.4 mile, just before the microwave towers, a sign shows the trail to the left, where it turns once more to dirt. A brief incline takes you to the top of a ridge that

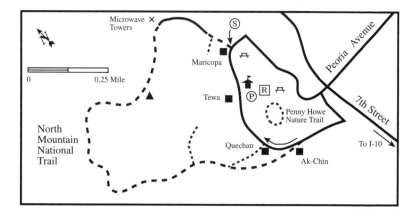

provides views of the surrounding area and where more desert plants like prickly pear cacti and thornbush await discovery.

During the hike, find a creosote bush close to the trail. Although it seems like just another common desert plant, it uses a secret weapon to help it grow better than all its neighbors. Its roots excrete a chemical that stops other plants from growing. The chemical stays in the soil until it is washed away by rain. Have the children look carefully around a creosote bush, because plants growing underneath it is a sign that the rainfall has been high.

A tenth of a mile along the ridge, just before the trail begins to descend, an outcropping of white quartz attracts the eye because it is so white compared to the black volcanic rock that lies everywhere. Older children can test the white rocks with their pocketknife to see if they really are quartz. A knife will not scratch quartz; it is too hard.

At 0.8 mile the trail passes behind the mountain peak, which entirely blocks the view of the city and park office. The peace and solitude on this section of the trail provides the atmosphere of the wide-open desert in the middle of a major city. Rest quietly and wait for a lizard, bird, or rabbit to come out of hiding.

The trail continues up and down until, at the 1-mile mark, it descends past some large rocks to a fork. The path to the left goes directly to the ranger station. Stay straight on the National Trail and within 0.1 mile, a trail marker appears. The trail descends again to an intersection with another trail to the left, which leads to the Quechan picnic shelter. Younger hikers can take the shortcut to Quechan, while the stronger ones continue for another 0.4 mile to the end of the trail at the Ak-Chin sheltered picnic area.

From either picnic area, follow the road to the left, back to the parking area.

Southern Arizona

Towering slabs of granite dwarf 150-foot tall pine trees, Lemmon Rock Lookout Trail

29. Molino Trail

Location: Coronado National Forest–Santa Catalina
Difficulty: Easy
Distance: 2.6 miles round trip
Hiking time: 2 hours
Hikable: October–May
Elevation gain: 600 feet
Maps: USGS Agua Caliente Hill; Santa Catalina Trail and Recreation Map 1997

A perfect example of the Upper Sonoran Life Zone, the Molino Trail is best hiked in March or April when the abundant plants are in bloom. The beauty and proximity of each plant encourages touching and investigation. The agave, mesquite, yucca, and prickly pear cactus all sport beautiful blooms. There are numerous dry washes to cross, two of which are deep and add the feeling of adventure to the terrain. Stay alert for bluebirds, lizards, and lichens on the rocks. There are bathrooms and water at the campground entrance.

Driving Instructions: From Interstate 10 in Tucson, take East Grant Road east 10 miles to the Tanque Verde Road intersection. Turn left onto Tanque Verde Road and travel 2 miles, then turn left onto Catalina Highway. Drive 9 miles to Molino Basin Campground just past mile marker 6. Turn left into the campground and follow the road to the end. The trailhead, elevation 4,400 feet, is just behind the last campsite. The trail is marked with a white Arizona Trail emblem on a brown fiberglass post.

A deep ravine lies within 200 feet of the trailhead. The water that flows in the wash during the wet season fosters large bushes of palmer oak. See if children can find their roundish acorns with a point on one end on the trail. Another 200 feet brings you to another wash with a concrete slab in the bottom. The amount of grass growing in the washes and around the trail indicates yearly rainfall of about 20 inches.

The trail continues with some ups and downs through one more wash until at 0.25 mile a dense thicket of manzanita is spotted. The leaves and bright red branches are so close and intertwined that it is impossible to see through the thicket to the other side. The white manzanita blossoms produce a reddish brown berry-like fruit that looks like a small apple. The plant was named for its fruit because manzanita means "small apple" in Spanish. Thickets of manzanita prevent erosion. Manzanita's small leaves help it survive the desert heat and years of drought by limiting the amount of moisture it transpires.

The trail continues past prickly pear cactus, lizards warming themselves on rocks, and alligator juniper. Have the children stop and look at an alligator juniper tree. It is the largest juniper species in Arizona. A single tree has an average life span of between 500 and 800 years, with the oldest ones living up to 1,400 years. There is movement along the trail as bluebirds fly from bush to bush in their search for food.

The trail continues up and down many small hills until a steady climb starts at 0.7 mile. Children can inspect any rock on the trail to study closely any lichens it may harbor. Lichens grow so slowly that their growth is measured in inches per century. Then have the children look up at the rough, rocky mountains to the left to see their greenish color. Talk about the centuries of growth necessary to see the green lichens on the barren rock from such a distance.

Switchbacks steadily climb the hill to a 270-degree turn in the trail at 0.8 mile. Watch for the airy, delicate leaves of the velvet mesquite in washes. Mesquite is a member of the pea family. As a legume, it returns nitrogen to the soil, enriching it for other plants. Its bean fruit ripens in the fall and is eaten by coyotes. Its roots burrow into the ground 5 feet in search of water.

The small summit at 1.2 miles provides a break from the climb and an opportunity to look at the small pinyon pine trees next to the trail. The nuts from the cones are edible and it is the most drought-resistant pine in Arizona. A fork in the road at 1.3 miles is marked with Arizona Trail emblems that show the Sycamore Reservoir Trail

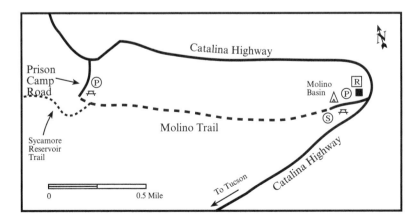

to the left; stay on the Molino Trail. Within a few hundred feet, Prison Camp picnic area comes into view. This makes a good lunch spot.

After a rest, return to Molino Basin Campground by the same route.

---

30. Sycamore Reservoir Trail

Location: Coronado National Forest–Santa Catalina
Difficulty: Moderate
Distance: 5.4 miles round trip
Hiking time: 4.5 hours
Hikable: October–May
Elevation gain: 600 feet
Maps: USGS Agua Caliente Hill, USGS Sabino Canyon; Santa Catalina Trail and Recreation Map 1997

Think of a picnic under tall, green, deciduous trees and cool shade surrounded by prickly pear cactus, manzanita, and agave. Sycamore Reservoir Trail leads to such an oasis. The hike traverses an abandoned road where remains of foundations, twisted pipes, and concrete pylons, all from the old Federal Prison Camp, spark children's imaginations. Birds flit between scrub oak and juniper bushes, while an occasional baby pinyon pine tree causes everyone to wonder how something so small gets so big. Large cypress trees, usually near rough washes, offer infrequent shade along the winding path down to the reservoir. A patio-like area offers a place to rest and look at the water that flows over the old spillway. Leaf rubbings make it easy to compare the difference between desert and riparian plants.

Driving Instructions: From Interstate 10 in Tucson, take East Grant Road east 10 miles to the Tanque Verde Road intersection. Turn left onto Tanque Verde Road, travel 2 miles, and turn left onto Catalina Highway. Drive 12 miles to the Prison Camp turnoff to the left. Park your car at the front of the picnic area and proceed on foot 100 feet to a tree that has a circular wall of stone, about 1.5 feet high, built around it. The trail begins here, elevation 5,000 feet.

Behind the tree, climb the wide trail up the hill and follow it as it veers to the right. Within 250 feet it crosses through a wash, then continues around the Prison Camp area. The first fork in the wide trail comes at 0.12 mile, where a sign shows the path on the left is the Molino Trail (hike 29); the right-hand path is the correct one for this hike. The trail is well marked with the Arizona Trail emblem on brown fiberglass poles.

At 0.25 mile, the trail turns into an old road as it enters a wide, open area. Several concrete foundations are all that remain from a Federal Prison Camp that housed inmates from 1939 until 1967. It may seem strange that a prison was built in such a remote region, but it housed the prisoners who built the road from Tucson to the top of Mount Lemmon. It took 8,000 inmates a little more than eleven years to complete the 25-mile stretch. In 1967, the camp was closed because it was too expensive to operate as a prison, and in 1973 the fifty-five abandoned buildings were razed by the Forest Service.

Just past the old foundations, the road forks once again. The fork to the left leads to the trailhead for Soldiers Trail #706, but continue straight, along a low stone structure that looks like a bridge, over a shallow wash. Within a few hundred feet, another Arizona Trail marker verifies that you are on the correct path.

The road leads to another fork at 0.5 mile, where you ignore the right branch and continue straight ahead to cross a small wash that then runs parallel to the road. Cypress, oak, and manzanita grow alongside the road, but its width makes them seem far away. With the children, look closely at the remnants of old, twisted metal pipes that lie alongside the road. The rust on their outer surfaces shows how nature's powerful forces returns everything to its base state. Beargrass appears as the road crosses a rocky, dry wash. Its long leaves are eaten by animals during drought, but they can be poisonous

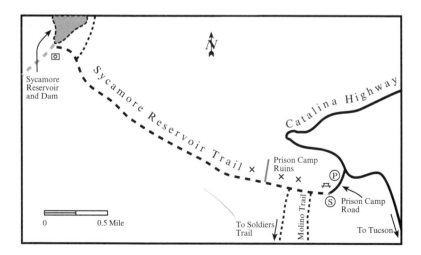

to sheep. Several other forks off of the main trail beckon the traveler, but always stay straight on the main road.

An Arizona Trail sign marks the trail at 0.85 mile. Birds fly between trees and bushes as they call to other birds. Small pine trees grow next to the road, while dead flower stalks from century plants dot the hills like swords pointing upward. At the 1-mile point, the road begins a climb that continues for 0.3 mile to the saddle at the mouth of Sycamore Canyon. A large sign explains the Arizona Trail system, while a smaller one marks where the Sycamore Reservoir Trail enters the Pusch Ridge Wilderness Area and descends to the reservoir. The now-narrow trail passes several four-sided, pyramid-shaped pillars of concrete and stones cemented together. Ask children what they think these are and why they are there. (They are the old pylons that held the pipes that brought water from the reservoir to the prison camp.)

On the other side of the rocky wash at 1.5 miles, a near-round boulder 6 feet in diameter sits on the right side of the trail. There are not that many boulders in the area. Have the children look around to see where it might have come from. Then have them look closely at the rock itself. It is either a highly eroded volcanic rock or a sedimentary rock pushed up from a lower layer by volcanic forces. Also have children look for desert plants and take rubbings of their leaves by putting a piece of paper over a leaf and rubbing a pencil lightly over the paper until the shape of the leaf appears. Save the rubbings for the end of the trail.

At the fork about 2 miles into the hike, don't take the right-hand path but stay straight and follow the trail as it veers to the right. Within a few hundred feet, the trail rejoins the old road that once led to the reservoir. As the road descends, the lush green of the many plants growing around the water comes into view. It is a contrast to the sparser desert plants on the nearby mountains. Near the trees, the trail goes either to the right around the reservoir or to the left to go to the actual dam. Stay to the left.

A small wall soon appears on the right and a concrete patio-like structure lies ahead. The patio closest to the spillway is walled, so it is possible to see the spillway without any danger. The dam spans a narrow canyon between two small mountains of dark volcanic rock. The reservoir has filled with sand over years of neglect, but spring runoff produces a roar as water careens over the spillway. The riparian cottonwood and oak trees offer deep shade in which to rest and enjoy a rare oasis and the desert all in the same view.

Have the children take leaf rubbings of the deciduous trees around the reservoir and compare them to the rubbings from the desert plants. The first obvious difference is the size of the leaves. The large deciduous leaves quickly lose moisture when it is hot. If the spring water did not continually feed the deciduous trees, they would quickly dehydrate and die. Desert plants have small leaves to retain water. Good rubbings also reveal large veins in the riparian leaves; the desert leaves, however, have few veins and waxy coatings. The small size and waxy coating of the desert plant leaves drastically slow water loss from where it is stored in the plants' branches. A desert plant can store water with very little loss through its leaves for a long time, enabling it to survive droughts.

When you are ready to leave the cool shade, return along the same path to your car.

31. Mount Lemmon and Lemmon Rock Lookout Trails

Location: Coronado National Forest–Santa Catalina
Difficulty: Easy
Distance: 1.6 miles round trip
Hiking time: 2 hours
Hikable: May-October
Elevation gain: 200 feet
Maps: USGS Mt. Lemmon; Santa Catalina Trail and Recreation Map 1997

From the trail, the Lemmon Rock fire lookout shack looks like a quaint cabin surrounded by trees. A closer look reveals a small, lone building on a huge, barren rock that commands the view of the entire area, including Tucson. Craggy mountain peaks and thick forests in the valleys combine for an inspiring view. Children enjoy exploring the many levels of Lemmon Rock, but they must be watched because there are no railings. The tall pine trees and high elevation make the hike pleasant in the summer. Squirrels race through the forest blanketed with bracken, a member of the fern family. The different types of pinecones along the trail are wonderful discoveries for young naturalists.

Driving Instructions: From Interstate 10 in Tucson, take East Grant Road east 10 miles to the Tanque Verde Road intersection. Turn left onto Tanque Verde Road, travel 2 miles, and turn left onto Catalina Highway. Stay on the highway as it climbs to 8,000 feet,

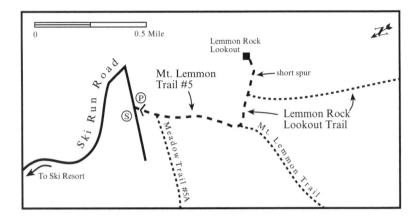

then descends slightly to Ski Run Road, which is also the road to Ski Valley, in 26 miles. Turn right onto Ski Run Road, continue past the ski resort, and go through two open gates to the end of the road and a parking area next to a power station surrounded by a high fence. The trail, elevation 9,000 feet, starts to the left of the power station as you face it; just follow the signs.

From the parking area, walk down the left side of the fenced power station, and at the back corner take the trail to the right, which leads to an open area. The plant growth is heavy just behind the station. Most of the plants are representative of what is seen on the rest of the trail, except for the quaking aspens. There are entire stands of quaking aspen on other parts of Mount Lemmon, so the few that grow near this trail are just samples. Have the children watch their leaves carefully. Whenever they move, see if you can feel any wind on your face. Chances are that the leaves will flutter even though you do not feel any air movement, because they quake at the merest hint of a breeze.

From the open area, veer left as the narrow trail widens to a dirt road that is the start of the Mount Lemmon Trail #5. Go around the gate blocking the road a few hundred feet past the clearing. The presence of many radio towers has given the area the name Radio Ridge. At night, the lights on the towers form a red blinking wall, but during the day they are difficult to see through the tall pine trees.

The rocks along the way, whose sizes range from minuscule grains

Stairs up to Lemmon Rock Lookout

of sand up to huge boulders, display a variety of reds, blacks, and grays mingled with shining bits of mica. Some of the prettiest rocks are swirls of light red and white of metamorphic origins. Often you will hear birds singing in the trees and see Albert or tassel-eared squirrels slowly walk through the thick pine needles of the forest floor in search of food. The trail descends until the first trail sign and intersection at 0.15 mile, where Meadow Trail #5A takes off to the right. Stay straight.

The road winds through stands of ponderosa pine and Douglas fir that rise high above a carpet of bracken. Point out to your children the long needles of the ponderosa pine and the short needles of the Douglas fir. Pinecones are the best evidence of the tree's species. The scales of the ponderosa cones are open, with triangular, pointed ends, while the Douglas fir cones have rounded scales that fit close together, with pointed bracts sticking out between them. Other cones suggest that there are also spruce trees hiding in the stand.

At 0.5 mile, the trail that forks to the left is Lemmon Rock Lookout Trail #12; take this left-hand trail that leads to Lemmon Rock. A short 0.1 mile later, another trail sign shows the Lemmon Rock Lookout Trail #12 going off to the right. Don't take this right-hand trail, but continue straight ahead on the short spur trail to the lookout. The view shows an opening in the trees about 1,100 feet away where the blue sky shows through.

As you continue, the very end of Lemmon Rock appears between the trees. The rock looks like a minor affair until you climb the stairs cut into the stone to the top of the rock, where the view opens to show the rest of a massive granite slab that commands an unparalleled view of vast forest, stony mountains, and flat, distant desert. It is clear why the location has been used to spot fires since 1902. The lookout itself is a small wooden building built in the 1920s. The view also reveals other enormous granite projections jutting vertically up between the pines of the forest. One of them is called Rappel Rock because it is a favorite spot for mountain climbers.

There is another set of stairs that leads to another small, flat porch. Let children explore the stairs and around the sides of the rock, but stay with them because there are no railings for protection. Have the children touch the rock to feel the texture of granite. Wrap your arms around as much of the rock as possible to try to get some idea of its size. Ask your children how rocks of such huge size are formed. Then tell them that the massive granite stones of Lemmon Rock formed when a large batholith of magma slowly cooled underground. Erosion over the centuries exposed the rocks without breaking them into smaller pieces.

After exploring and enjoying the area, return along the same route.

32. Mount Lemmon, Lemmon Rock Lookout, and Wilderness of Rocks Trails

Location: Coronado National Forest–Santa Catalina
Difficulty: Strenuous
Distance: 9.3-mile loop
Hiking time: 7 hours
Hikable: May-October
Elevation gain: 1,900 feet
Maps: USGS Mt. Lemmon; Santa Catalina Trail and Recreation Map 1997

The length and large change in altitude makes this day hike into the Wilderness of Rocks an adventure suitable for older children. The trail

An enormous pine tree

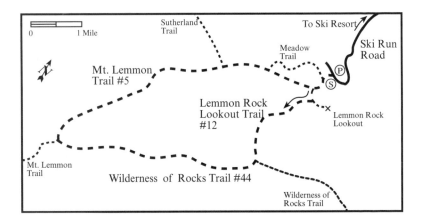

starts in thick forest carpeted with pine needles and bracken. Switchbacks down Mount Lemmon lead through a potpourri of stony washes, sculpted rocks, and groves of tall pines. Sections of the trail are solid stone surrounded by weird-shaped rocks, making the terrain look more lunar than earthly. Piles of boulders among the trees make the landscape unique. Pleasant surprises along the way include horny toads, carpenter ants, and fallen trees that have been cut so their rings can be counted. Many parts of the trail are shaded, so it is a perfect hike for the summer. Take all your own water.

Driving Instructions: From Interstate 10 in Tucson, take East Grant Road east 10 miles to the Tanque Verde Road intersection. Turn left onto Tanque Verde Road, travel 2 miles, and turn left onto Catalina Highway. Stay on the highway as it climbs to 8,000 feet, then descends slightly, to Ski Run Road in 26 miles, which is also the road to Ski Valley. Turn right onto Ski Run Road, continue past the ski resort, and go through two open gates to the end of the road and a parking area next to a power station surrounded by a high fence. The trail, elevation 9,000 feet, starts to the left of the power station as you face it; just follow the signs.

The first 0.6 mile of the hike follows the route of hike 31, Mount Lemmon and Lemmon Rock Lookout Trails (see that trail description). At the signed intersection where Lemmon Rock is straight ahead on a short spur trail and Lemmon Rock Lookout Trail #12 peels off to the right, go right to stay on Lemmon Rock Lookout Trail. The trail immediately begins a fairly steep descent along switchbacks through crowded trees that provide cool shade. Pinecones in abundance lie among the grasses that grow under the trees. The large boulders that occasionally jut up seem out of place in a conifer forest.

At 0.75 mile, a tree has fallen over the trail. Have the children look closely at the two types of moss growing on it as you pass under. Watch also for the narrowleaf penstemon, a purple wildflower that looks like a snapdragon. Compare the sizes of the trees and look for the giants that are so big that adults cannot put their arms around even half of the circumference.

A dead tree about 50 feet long lies along the trail at 1.4 miles. Walk along the tree, then have everyone lie head-to-toe next to it in a line to try to get an idea of its size. Near the dead tree is a large ponderosa pine. Have the children follow it with their eyes from its base to the very top, and compare it to the tree on the ground. The trees of the forest are tall; many approach 130 feet, which is about the height of a ten-story building. Another large dead tree 0.1 mile later shows the thick, strong roots it takes to bolt these giants to the earth.

A trail through tall pines and large granite boulders

The trail now descends rapidly, with fewer switchbacks, through more frequent and larger piles of rocks until it reaches a signed intersection at 2.6 miles. Take the right fork, Wilderness of Rocks Trail #44, to enter a land that alternates between stands of pine trees and areas of solid rock of strange, eroded shapes. The 1,700-foot decline in altitude from the trailhead adds claret cup cactus, Schott agave, and yucca to the list of plants to discover. Remind children to be observant because it is not uncommon to see lizards, horny toads, and snakes as they search for a warm place to lie.

The trail varies from packed earth to solid stone, with small elevation changes. Rock cairns mark all areas where the easily visible, packed-earth trail metamorphoses into solid rock. Tell the children to look carefully around any dead logs for sawdust, a sign that carpenter ants are busy at work.

An opening in the trees, at 2.9 miles, provides a good view of Rappel Rock, Lemmon Rock, and the other huge granite stones protruding through the trees. Granite is an intrusive volcanic rock, which means that it was hot magma that never flowed through a volcano opening to the surface above. Mount Lemmon was once a massive magma chamber that slowly cooled under the earth and formed granite. Erosion removed the outer layer of dirt and over the years carved the exposed stone into columns that look like building blocks left behind by giants after play.

At 3.3 miles, 15 feet of the trail is a groove eroded into the rock, and at 3.6 miles, the absence of any plant life and the presence of strange rocks give an almost lunar look to the area. The best opportunity for children to count the rings on a tree occurs where the trail climbs around an 80-foot-tall black boulder at 4 miles.

At the T intersection with the Mount Lemmon Trail #5, at 5.1 miles, go to the right onto the Mount Lemmon Trail. This point marks the last leg of the hike and the start of a nearly continuous climb. Boulders are numerous for the next mile, with one that looks like a model boat on a stand to the left of the trail at 5.8 miles. Breaks in the trees offer glimpses of Tucson in the distance and other gray, bald mountains nearby. Take a rest from the steady climb to look for ladybugs on the plants. Just for fun, see who can find the first one without any spots on its wings.

Switchbacks cut once more through forest with bracken and wildflowers. The Sutherland Trail intersects at 7.7 miles; stay right, on the Mount Lemmon Trail. A stand of quaking aspens wave hello a short 0.5 mile later. In an additional 0.5 mile, there is a view of the top of Rappel Rock to the right and, shortly after that, an intersection with Meadow Trail on the left.

At the junction with Lemmon Rock Lookout Trail #12 at 8.8 miles, go left to stay on the Mount Lemmon Trail. This intersection marks familiar territory, with a moderate climb of 0.5 mile back to the car. A single hike has taken you from the lush green of conifer forests to nature's art studio filled with carved stone masterpieces, then all the way back to the start.

33. Incinerator Ridge Trail

Location: Coronado National Forest–Santa Catalina
Difficulty: Easy
Distance: 3 miles round trip
Hiking time: 2.5 hours
Hikable: May-October
Elevation gain: 150 feet
Maps: USGS Mt. Bigelow; Santa Catalina Trail and Recreation Map 1997

Glittering rocks, tiny gambel oak bushes, large trees shaped like slingshots, horny toads, and gopher holes make this short hike to the end of Incinerator Ridge an adventure of exploration for children of all ages. Other wonders along the trail are eroding granite boulders that crumble at the touch like aged blue cheese and a single, hidden claret cup cactus. Except for a few hundred feet, the entire trail is shaded by tall pine trees that make it a nice summer hike.

Driving Instructions: From Interstate 10 in Tucson, take East Grant Road east 10 miles to the Tanque Verde Road intersection. Turn left onto Tanque Verde Road, travel 2 miles, and turn left onto Catalina Highway. Stay on the highway, and go past Incinerator Ridge Road at 22 miles to the parking lot directly opposite the Palisade Visitors Center. Park your car in the lot, which is the starting point of the hike, elevation 7,900 feet. (Alternatively, a high-clearance vehicle can easily drive the Incinerator Ridge Road. From the Catalina Highway, take a right onto Incinerator Ridge Road and drive to the end of the road. This reduces the hike to 1 mile round trip and, although a lot of treasures are missed, it is a nice option for very small children.)

From the Palisade Visitors Center parking lot, stay on the same side of the road as the parking lot and begin to walk back along

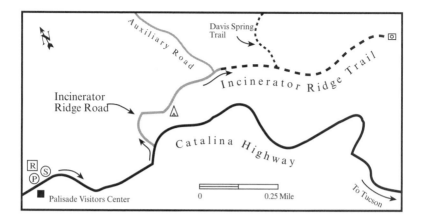

Catalina Highway to Incinerator Ridge Road. The wide shoulder provides plenty of room to stay off the road, but keep an eye on children to make sure they are safe. After 0.5 mile of wildflowers, grasses, and small rock cliffs, turn left onto unpaved Incinerator Ridge Road and follow as it cuts into the forest. The road quickly rises along a gulch to the right, with large granite boulders to the left. Have the children inspect the boulders to see how the change from warm weather to freezing temperatures cracks the rock. When they touch the rocks, parts of the stone that look solid flake off in big, sand-like particles much like a brick of blue cheese crumbles to bits.

The road continues to climb through yewleaf willows and silverleaf oak until, at 0.65 mile, just before a sharp right turn in the road, a strange pine tree down in the gulch to the right appears. Its trunk rises from the ground for 30 feet, then suddenly splits in two and continues up as two separate trees, looking much like a gigantic slingshot. Tell the children to watch for other similar trees, because there are a few others along the way. They can also look for acorns from both the silverleaf and wavyleaf oaks that grow along the way. The egg-shaped acorns come from the silverleaf oak and have a tiny point on the end.

At 0.75 mile, a road to the right leads to a nice camping area, but stay straight and look for golden bearded penstemon flowers, which grow scattered in the undergrowth. The gated auxiliary road to the left at 0.95 mile is not the correct path, so stay to the right where, within 100 feet, you pass between two tree stumps to find the end

Long-dead pine on Incinerator Ridge

Father and son enjoying the Incinerator Ridge Trail

of the road and two trail signs. The first sign marks the trail as
Incinerator Ridge Trail #18A and the second relates that the end is
a mere 0.5 mile straight ahead. Just beyond the signs, the wide trail
passes by a community of gophers marked by mounds of dirt. Luxu-
riant grasses grow under pine trees that occasionally give way to the
right of the trail to a view of distant mountains covered with pines.
The view to the left shows an abrupt end of the mountains, followed
by a flat, endless plain. A few dead, tall pines stand as lonely sentinels among the new small pines that grow on the ridge.

At 1.1 miles, the trail turns sharply to the right and marks the
spot of another slingshot tree, but this time it has three trees growing
from the same trunk instead of two. Just past the tree is the intersection with the Davis Spring Trail to the left. Continue straight as
the Incinerator Ridge Trail ascends ever so gradually. Have the children
look closely near the thickets of gambel oak, crowded under the trees,

for baby oak plants that are nothing more than a tiny twig with full-sized leaves. Baby pine trees also show the beginning stages of what will become massive giants. The sparkle from the pretty golden-colored rocks along the trail invites children to touch and look more closely.

At 1.4 miles the trail narrows as it climbs through trees and reaches a peak 100 feet later. The trail disappears at the end near large rocks that are perfect for resting and enjoying the view. Rose Canyon Lake peeks through the trees on the right, and a large mine is visible on the desert plain to the left. Have the children look for the claret cup cactus that grows near a rock at the end of the trail, and also for horny toads warming themselves on rocks before the temperature falls once again with the setting sun.

Return along the same path.

34. Mount Bigelow Trail

Location: Coronado National Forest–Santa Catalina
Difficulty: Moderate
Distance: 2 miles round trip
Hiking time: 2 hours
Hikable: May-October
Elevation gain: 500 feet
Maps: USGS Mt. Bigelow; Santa Catalina Trail and Recreation Map 1997

Pine forests, blue butterflies, hundreds of ladybugs, and hummingbirds are all part of the short hike to the fire lookout tower on the top of Mount Bigelow. Suitable for even small children, the trail ascends past patches of catnip, large fallen trees, and rust-colored granite. The occasional gray rocks with swirling patterns make a fascinating geological find for young hikers. An excellent way to begin the hike is with a visit to the Palisade Visitors Center, and the only way to end it is to climb the fire lookout tower at the summit.

Driving Instructions: From Interstate 10 in Tucson, take East Grant Road east 10 miles to the Tanque Verde Road intersection. Turn left onto Tanque Verde Road, travel 2 miles, and turn left onto Catalina Highway. Stay on the highway, and drive 22 miles to the

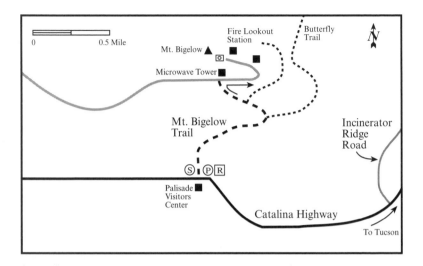

parking lot directly opposite the Palisade Visitors Center. The trailhead is at the upper end of the parking lot, elevation 7,900 feet.

Whether you explore the Visitors Center before or after the hike, do not miss the huge tree cross section, the relief model of Mount Lemmon, and the furs, skins, bones, and rocks that are displayed to be touched. The General Hitchcock tree, named after the man who organized the construction of the first road up Mount Lemmon, was a 125-foot-high, 300-year-old pine that was 7 feet in diameter at its base when it died in 1952. A 4-foot cross section from the tree has pins marking the rings corresponding to the Civil War, the Revolutionary War, and Father Kino's arrival in Arizona in 1694. The Mount Lemmon relief model allows hikers to touch sharp ridges, feel steep mountainsides, and trace winding mountain trails. The most exciting part is finding the trails you have already hiked. The tactile display has bones, skulls, and skins of common forest animals along with the glittering rocks found on the Mount Bigelow Trail. In the summer, hummingbirds visit the feeder hanging outside the back window, but they are also frequently sighted on the trail.

There are numerous signs at the trailhead but only one trail, which almost immediately starts an easy climb past green water tanks on the left. Pine needles, sparkling rocks, decomposed granite, grasses, and bracken form beautiful patterns on the forest floor under the tall pines. Within a few hundred feet of the trailhead, a large stump about 2.5 feet in diameter lies next to the trail. Although the children may have seen a lot of tree stumps and counted a lot of tree rings, the memory of the General Hitchcock tree might inspire them to look and count more closely.

Boulders infrequently dot the terrain until, at 0.1 mile, a 10-foot-high, 15-foot-long bump appears that is so covered with lichens that it is difficult to see the granite rock underneath. Lichens are a combination of a fungus and algae. Algae use photosynthesis to produce food to feed both itself and the fungus, while the fungus shields the algae from excessive ultraviolet rays. There are over 15,000 types of lichens, but this rock is mostly covered by only one type. See if the children can find a spot on the rock that is not covered by lichen.

The trail continues up the hill until at 0.2 mile there is a fork whose left path is blocked by small logs. Continue to the right past a massive boulder and watch for the pretty rust-red color that iron oxides gives to some of the granite rocks. Switchbacks continue up the mountain, passing large rocks and carpenter ants that slowly reduce dead trees to a honeycomb of tunnels and small piles of sawdust. The summer sun warms the air, but the tall trees protect the trail and provide coolness to the hundreds of ladybugs that children can find on bushes. Beautiful blue butterflies flutter from bush to bush, challenging amateur entomologists to identify them before they flutter out of range.

The easy ascent brings you to the intersection with the Butterfly Trail at 0.55 mile. Stay to the left on the Mount Bigelow Trail to reach Bigelow's summit. The valleys along the trail seem deep until compared to the even more formidable valleys revealed through openings in the tall trees. Granite rocks with mica in them litter the trail and glitter attractively. Encourage the children to pick one up and see how mica forms in thin layers that flake off.

The trail still climbs when, at 0.7 mile, it reaches an intersection marked by a large boulder; take the left fork. Just 250 feet up the left fork, the spread-out roots of a large fallen tree almost block the trail, forcing you to stoop as you walk under. The hard-packed dirt trail continues past yellow daisy flowers and penstemons to a T intersection with a service road next to a microwave tower. Enjoy the view of Tucson far below, then turn right onto the road and continue up it while searching for rocks with a gray swirling pattern.

The road curves to the left and passes a building, and then continues up a small trail to the right to arrive at a fire lookout tower at the 1-mile mark. Even when the tower is not open, guests can climb up part of the way to see what it is like to be a forest ranger on lookout duty. Strong gusts of wind cause the tower to sway noticeably, but most summer days are calm and the tower provides a beautiful vantage point from which to survey the thick forests below.

After you have enjoyed the spectacular views, return the same way you came.

35. Butterfly Peak

Location: Coronado National Forest–Santa Catalina
Difficulty: Moderate
Distance: 2.4 miles round trip
Hiking time: 2.5 hours
Hikable: May-October
Elevation gain: 470 feet
Maps: USGS Mt. Bigelow; Santa Catalina Trail and Recreation Map 1997

The beauty of the yellow columbine is not fully appreciated until it is seen in the company of crimson monkey flower, prostrate vervain, and golden bearded penstemon along the Butterfly Trail on the way to Butterfly Peak. The occasionally narrow forest trail descends past dead tree stumps with strangely shaped mushrooms, eroding rocks, thickets of gambel oak, beautiful butterflies collecting pollen, and a lone tree inflicted with mistletoe. Lofty pines provide deep shade for comfort on even the warmest summer days for most of the trail, except the last short ascent to the peak. Views along the way and at the peak reveal tall mountains covered with pine, with occasional outcroppings of enormous granite boulders. Carry a camera with color film for the flowers and the butterflies.

Driving Instructions: From Interstate 10 in Tucson, take East

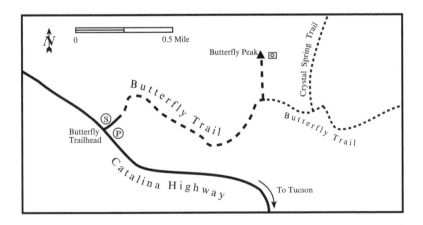

Grant Road east 10 miles to the Tanque Verde Road intersection. Turn left onto Tanque Verde Road, travel 2 miles, and turn left onto Catalina Highway. Stay on the highway just beyond mile marker 22, where a sign marks the parking area for the Butterfly Trail. The trail, elevation 7,700 feet, begins as a paved road at the end of the parking lot past a gate.

Note: Although the Butterfly Trail leads to Butterfly Peak (this hike), hike 36, Butterfly Trail, and hike 37, Crystal Spring Trail, also start from this same trailhead and share the Butterfly Trail for the first mile or so before each hike separates to its distinct destination.

A mere 100 feet down the paved road is the first dead tree stump with weird-shaped white mushrooms. Warm, damp weather is ideal for mushrooms, so during the storms of August, have the children watch for others along the trail. The gray-colored rock that forms a wall along the right of the road erodes in layers, so the exposed rock is uniformly patterned with small steps. Children can run a finger across an eroded face and see how the thickness of the layers is somewhere between ⅛ and ¼ inch.

Just before the asphalt ends, a pine tree grows out of the rock wall. Even from a distance it is clear that something is different about this tree. Have the children look closely to see mistletoe sprouting directly from the pine's branches. The mistletoe roots penetrate the bark, live off of the sap produced by the pine tree, and eventually kill the tree. Its seeds are spread by the birds that eat its berries.

Just past the asphalt, where the road forks stay to the left. The trail continues downward, in spite of some minor ascents, through pine trees to another fork at 0.15 mile. Once more, stay to the left and enjoy the occasional break in the trees that reveal nearby tall mountains covered with trees. Shortly after the fork, the trail narrows but continues through thick forest where it is hard to see the sweetly singing birds.

The gray color of a granite rock at 0.3 mile is broken by the red blossoms of the golden bearded penstemon flowers growing directly out of the stone. See if the children can look closely for roots plunging deep into the cracks in search of nourishment. At times the trail is narrow and lined by thickets of gambel oak. Thick black lines of ants gathering food from the forest floor clutter are easily seen. Children can follow an ant line to see the tree or rock where they live. At 0.5 mile, climb over the roots of an old, gnarled tree growing in the middle of the trail.

The trail crosses many valleys where folds of the mountain come together to form a natural drainage to carry rainwater from the slopes above. Rushing water has turned some valleys into deep gorges, while

The forest engulfs the trail on the way to Butterfly Peak.

others look almost tropical because of the plants that take advantage of the increased amounts of water. The trail curves at 0.7 mile through a beautiful drainage with an awe-inspiring variety of flowers. Encourage children to look closely at the yellow columbine with its big, open, star-like blossoms. Enjoy large patches of golden bearded penstemon that wave in the breeze and the crimson monkey flower that plays among the tiny purple flowers of the prostrate vervain. Savor the beauty that is seen and enjoyed only in the solitude of the deep forest.

Reluctantly, bid the wild beauties adieu and continue along the trail over other deep valleys to the wide intersection at the 1-mile point. The Butterfly Trail continues to the right; take the left fork, which is a short spur trail that leads to the top of Butterfly Peak.

As the trail begins to ascend the hill, the ground changes almost immediately from a layer of pine needles to rough boulders, and the packed dirt under foot, at points, becomes solid rock. The arid feel of the small knoll is intensified by the presence of yucca, manzanita, and lizards. The short climb tops out at 1.2 miles, where three trees block passage along the trail. Have children look for big beetles around the trees and claret cup cactus near the rocks, and enjoy the open views from the top of the small peak.

After descending Butterfly Peak, return along the same route you came on.

36. Butterfly Trail

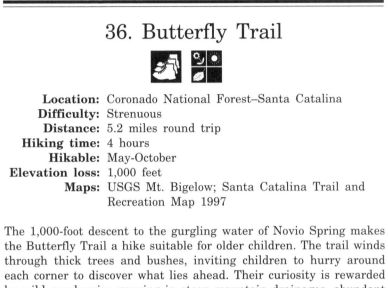

Location: Coronado National Forest–Santa Catalina
Difficulty: Strenuous
Distance: 5.2 miles round trip
Hiking time: 4 hours
Hikable: May-October
Elevation loss: 1,000 feet
Maps: USGS Mt. Bigelow; Santa Catalina Trail and Recreation Map 1997

The 1,000-foot descent to the gurgling water of Novio Spring makes the Butterfly Trail a hike suitable for older children. The trail winds through thick trees and bushes, inviting children to hurry around each corner to discover what lies ahead. Their curiosity is rewarded by wild raspberries growing in steep mountain drainages, abundant wildflowers, and chipmunks playing tag in the forest. The descent

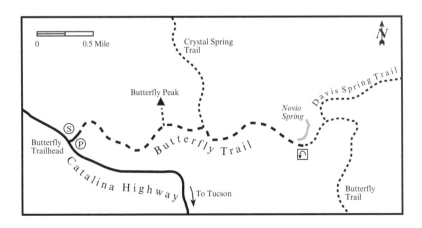

carries the hiker from pine trees into the desert environment where Schott's yucca thrives, then back into thick pine trees once again. The many pools of the spring offer children endless exploration to find tadpoles, water skeeters, and spiders. The water in Novio Spring flows the entire year except for the very hottest days of summer. Purify the water before drinking.

Driving Instructions: From Interstate 10 in Tucson, take East Grant Road east 10 miles to the Tanque Verde Road intersection. Turn left onto Tanque Verde Road, travel 2 miles, and turn left onto Catalina Highway. Stay on the highway just beyond mile marker 22, where a sign marks the parking area for the Butterfly Trail. The trail, elevation 7,700 feet, begins as a paved road at the end of the parking lot past a gate.

Note: Hike 35, Butterfly Peak; this hike, Butterfly Trail; and hike 37, Crystal Spring Trail, all start from this same trailhead and share the same trail—the Butterfly Trail—for the first mile or so before they separate to their distinct destinations.

Within a few hundred feet, the paved road turns into a wide dirt track that soon arrives at an intersection. Take the left fork as the level trail passes majestic trees up to 3 feet in diameter and tracks a deep ravine. At the intersection at 0.15 mile, again take the left fork where the broad road narrows to a single-file mountain trail and begins to descend the side of the steep mountain through tall pines with thick undergrowth. Help the children notice how several mountain ash trees next to the large rock at 0.25 mile seem to grow out of a common root system. Have children look closely at the tunnel spider webs in the rough bark of the ponderosa pines to see if their shy occupants will make an appearance.

The trail frequently crosses valleys between ridges that drain water from the mountain. Fast-running water has cut deep ravines in some valleys, and in others has formed areas where plants, including wild raspberries and flowers, grow abundantly. The drainage at 0.4 mile supplies enough water for the bigtooth maple to grow and later, at 0.9 mile, thick patches of oak and maple shade the trail. The broad intersection at the 1-mile mark provides access to Butterfly Peak to the left, but for this hike, take the right fork to continue on the Butterfly Trail's descent past thick summer bracken toward Novio Springs.

Only 0.2 mile after the intersection, the thick forest surrounding the meandering trail cloaks each twist in mystery and encourages young hikers to rush to see what lies ahead. The thick undergrowth abates and a clearing forms near the intersection with Crystal Springs Trail at 1.4 miles. Stay straight, on the Butterfly Trail, as yucca and silverleaf and wavyleaf oak become more abundant. At 1.6 miles, the trail becomes less clear as it begins to cross a dry streambed, but a

Along the Butterfly Trail

large pine tree and a rock cairn mark the way and the trail soon becomes well defined once more. The steep descent of the trail, which is rocky at times, is mitigated by switchbacks that cut through thickets of gambel oak, across gorges, and past large granite boulders among the trees.

A warmer, less shaded section of the trail, at 2 miles, allows yucca to thrive and invites lizards to warm themselves on the rocks, but the thick forest returns a mere 0.4 mile later. When you are once again in the forest, butterflies flutter, birds call to their friends, and chipmunks play in the trees; then at 2.5 miles, an immense black rock rises next to the trail. Walk through the depression at its base, which fills with water when it rains, and past the rock to an intersection a few hundred feet later. The left fork leads down a hill to pools of water, but continue straight 0.1 mile as the road begins to parallel the small stream formed by the springs.

A turnoff to the waters of Novio Springs is marked by a large fallen tree to the right of the trail and a 3-foot-high rock that is almost square and nearly 4 feet across. Take the path to the left, just beyond the boulder, down to the jumble of rocks that form myriad small pools of clear water at different levels. Children love to explore to find water skeeters, tadpoles, spiders, and moss. In late summer, the flow is low, but the constant gurgle announces that water is slowly flowing over rocks from the higher to the lower pools. Can the children find where the water leaves one pool and enters another?

After you have enjoyed the deep shade and the serenity of the remote spring, return along the same path.

37. Crystal Spring Trail

Location:	Coronado National Forest–Santa Catalina
Difficulty:	Strenuous
Distance:	6.2 miles round trip
Hiking time:	5 hours
Hikable:	May-October
Elevation loss:	920 feet
Maps:	USGS Mt. Bigelow; Santa Catalina Trail and Recreation Map 1997

True mountain trails lead to miniature Crystal Spring, so quaint it could be right out of a Norman Rockwell painting. Thick forests generously coated with pine needles and warm southern slopes populated with Schott's yucca are the trail's companions as it climbs high over a rough, dry drainage. Narrow at times, occasionally steep, and continuously winding, the trail passes fallen giant trees slowly transforming into the rich, dark humus that supports areas of thick grasses and heavy undergrowth. Alligator juniper, granite boulders, and square spider webs lie along Crystal Spring Trail on the way to the picturesque spring. Because the spring is small and unreliable, take all the water you will need.

Driving Instructions: From Interstate 10 in Tucson, take East Grant Road east 10 miles to the Tanque Verde Road intersection. Turn left onto Tanque Verde Road, travel 2 miles, and turn left onto Catalina Highway. Stay on the highway until just beyond mile marker 22, where a sign marks the parking area for the Butterfly Trail. The trail, elevation 7,700 feet, begins as a paved road at the end of the parking lot past a gate.

Note: Hike 35, Butterfly Peak, and hike 36, Butterfly Trail, also start from this same trailhead and share the same trail—the Butterfly Trail—for the first mile or so before they separate to their distinct destinations. The Crystal Spring Trail takes off from the Butterfly Trail 1.4 miles from the Butterfly Trailhead.

From the Butterfly Trailhead, the pavement quickly ends and the broad dirt road arrives at an intersection within 200 feet. Follow the road to the left until it comes to another intersection at 0.15 mile. Take the left fork as the trail narrows and descends through thick forest, deep valleys, and infrequent, large granite rocks. Have children look for the tree that fell across the trail at 0.4 mile but was cut in two to provide passage. Children can closely search the tree's rotting interior for the bugs and fungi that transform these fallen giants into rich soil waiting to nourish anything that will grow. Notice that carpenter ants chewed parts of the once-solid tree into a delicate, wooden lace. Just past the rotting tree are two live pines whose trunks, growing from common roots, form a V shape.

The narrow trail winds past valleys cut deep by rushing waters and drainages choked with plants and wildflowers. The mountain rises steeply to one side of the trail and drops off, just as quickly, on the other side. The exposed tree roots and man-made embankments show that the trail is battered by the elements and could easily be wiped away by the powerful rush of water from a single violent storm, but such thoughts are spirited away by the soft breeze through the trees and the dapple of warm sunlight on the calm,

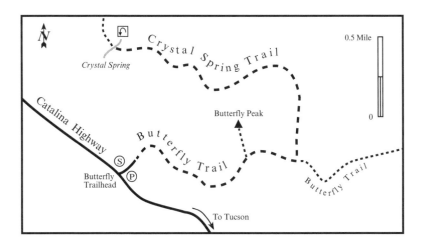

summer forest floor. Elderberry trees and yucca plants are seen at the 0.85-mile point.

The trail descends to the intersection at the 1-mile mark; the left fork is a short spur trail to Butterfly Peak. Continue straight on the Butterfly Trail; at the 1.3-mile point, the hard, decay-resistant knots from branches are about all that remains from another rotting tree. See if children can find spider webs spun between tree branches, looking like square handkerchiefs waiting to engulf anything that might fly by.

The signed intersection at 1.4 miles shows that Crystal Spring Trail descends to the left; take this fork through a thick stand of pines carpeted by bracken and a thick layer of needles. At 1.5 miles, another immense dead tree, whose gnarled branches still twist in every direction, lies to the left. Thick undergrowth crowds the trail along a 250-foot stretch where the increased southern exposure changes the plant mix from all ponderosa pines to gambel oaks, huge alligator junipers, yuccas, silverleaf oaks, and even century plants.

The trail winds, rises, and falls through patches of thick bushes and rocky, barren areas until at 2.1 miles it descends, over loose dirt, along a huge stone wall 200 feet long and 75 feet high. Only 0.2 mile later, the flora is once again thick pines with bracken on the floor, singing birds in the canopy, and fallen trees silently turning to earth. Enjoy the cool shade and the bright colors of flowers dotted under the pines. Also keep a close eye on the trail because, at 2.4 miles, two recently fallen trees obscure and block passage. Work your way around the trees and the trail becomes clear again.

There are several notable milestones along the next stretch of the trail, which pique children's curiosity. There are so many little mysteries and never enough time to fully investigate (but here are a few hints). At 2.5 miles a fallen tree's long, exposed roots twist in all directions. Why did the strong roots fail to keep the tree upright? (During wet years, trees can more easily be uprooted because the ground is not as hard and does not hold the tree as tightly as when it is dry.) At 2.7 miles a large, moss-covered rock rests at a sharp right turn in the trail. Why is the rock covered with moss when there is no apparent water to maintain it? (Some mosses only need occasional rains to survive.) Just past it, a huge boulder 70 feet tall by 200 feet around lies close by in the forest. How was such a large boulder left with no others beside it? (The boulder could have been simply a vent of magma that hardened before it could make it to the surface.)

Once again you are reminded of nature's awesome power when the trail crosses a dry streambed, then climbs along the edge of the deep gorge cut by rushing waters. From the top of the ascent, the gorge appears so deep and the valley in the distance so open and untouched that children feel like explorers stepping into an entirely new land. The trail begins a sharp ascent at 3.1 miles and, just as it levels out, a tree appears growing on the left edge of the trail. The moist depression in front of the tree seems most ordinary until you notice a weathered, wooden sign leaning at an angle against the exposed roots with faded letters that spell Crystal Spring. Although water does not bubble from the spring, it is not hard to picture an old forest ranger with a white beard and worn shoes or a group of young Boy Scouts resting next to it. What a quaint picture it makes.

Take a rest yourself, then return by the same path.

38. Valley View Overlook Trail

Location: Saguaro National Park West
Difficulty: Easy
Distance: 0.6 mile round trip
Hiking time: 0.5 hour
Hikable: Year-round
Elevation gain: 240 feet
Map: USGS Avra

The entire Saguaro National Park West area is a living museum of Lower Sonoran plant life, with the saguaro cactus as its centerpiece.

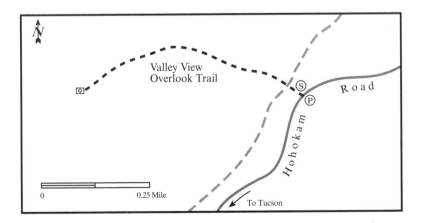

Healthy saguaro cacti at all stages of development represent hundreds of years of growth. Young saguaro cacti's dependence on other plants is clearly demonstrated. Black lines of ants carry cactus fruit many times larger than themselves back to their nests for consumption. Holes in the saguaro, drilled by the gila woodpecker, as well as burrows underground house a variety of desert animals. Stop in the Visitors Center to see a marvelous display of animals and their habitats before starting the hike. The trail ends at a Park Service display that overlooks a broad valley filled with saguaro. The display has a photograph taken in 1890 of the same valley.

Driving Instructions: From Interstate 10 in Tucson, exit onto westbound State Highway 86, also known as the Ajo-Tucson Highway. Follow it 6 miles to the right turn onto Kinney Road. Stay on Kinney Road until it enters Saguaro National Park West, passes the Visitors Center, and intersects Hohokam Road in approximately 12 miles. Turn right onto the dirt Hohokam Road and drive to the sign that marks the trailhead, elevation 2,620 feet. The parking is just off the road.

Right from the trailhead, hikers receive a greeting from the bounties of desert life. Even though the plant life seems sparse compared to growth in an Arizonan pine forest, look carefully around at the variety, proximity, and amount of each species. If you consciously identify the compass cactus, prickly pear cactus, paloverde trees, creosote bush, teddy bear cholla, mesquite, ocotillo, sagebrush, pencil cholla, desert lavender, hedgehog cactus, silver cholla, and of course the saguaro, you have only noticed a fraction of the plants. Look for lines of black ants laboriously carrying comparatively huge fruit from the cacti back to their homes in the ground. Notice the holes under bushes that are just big enough for a snake, lizard, or pack rat to use as an entrance to their underground abode. Find holes drilled in the saguaro cacti by the gila woodpecker, which inhabit these homes. The desert is full of life. Attune your senses, and its beauty and vibrancy becomes apparent.

Just past the sandy wash 200 feet from the trailhead, have children search for the tiny saguaro cacti that are between 1 inch and 1 foot tall. It is hard to believe, but young saguaro cacti cannot bear the heat of the direct sun. Small saguaros are always found under a bush, such as paloverde or creosote, that is known as a nurse plant, protecting the tender cacti from direct sunlight. Saguaro populations are severely impacted when the nurse plants are destroyed. As the saguaro gets taller, it grows right up through its nurse plant's branches. That is why there are so many saguaros growing right next to creosote bushes and paloverde trees.

Look also for saguaro that are between 1 and 2 feet tall. They

Sweetheart saguaro cacti enjoy the view together.

A view from Valley View Overlook reveals hundreds of saguaro cactus.

look like upside-down bowling pins because their bases are smaller than their tops. Most adult saguaro have the rounded top that is so commonly seen, but the tops of some saguaro cacti fan out and grow in strange, beautiful patterns. Cacti with such strange crowns are known as "cristated"; unfortunately, there are none of these along the trail. These cristated cacti are rare and no one understands why they grow the way they do.

The trail ascends to a small plateau at 0.3 mile where there is a picture, taken in 1890, of the area it overlooks. Children can judge for themselves whether there are more saguaro cacti today than there were more than 100 years ago. In the winter and during the monsoon season, clouds darken the sky and make the distant mountains look ominous. If the wind is blowing, have the children look carefully at the larger saguaros. The thick roots of each cactus spread far to find water, but usually not too deep, so the cacti noticeably sway in stronger winds.

Enjoy the marvelous view, then return along the same trail.

39. Signal Hill Trail

Location: Saguaro National Park West
Difficulty: Easy
Distance: 0.25 mile round trip
Hiking time: 0.5 hour or less
Hikable: Year-round
Elevation gain: 30 feet
Map: USGS Avra

This is the perfect hike for little children because it is short, easy, and loaded with things to discover, see, and sometimes touch. Giant compass cacti, prickly pear cacti with bite marks, a stone dam, pencil cholla, and a rock with a beautiful swirling pattern are all part of the climb up the small Signal Hill to see black basalt rocks covered with white petroglyphs. The picnic tables and grills near the trailhead make it convenient to combine the hike with a picnic.

Driving Instructions: From Interstate 10 in Tucson, exit onto westbound State Highway 86, also known as the Ajo-Tucson Highway. Follow it 6 miles to the right turn onto Kinney Road. Stay on Kinney Road as it enters Saguaro National Park West, passes the Visitors Center, and intersects Hohokam Road in approximately 12 miles. Turn right onto the dirt Hohokam Road, and at Golden Gate Road, turn left and drive almost all the way around the loop to the

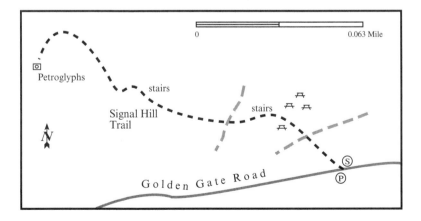

sign that marks the trailhead. Parking is just off of the road, elevation 2,400 feet.

Signal Hill, visible from the trailhead, is the destination but before starting, have the children look at the compass cactus near the trailhead and remember its size so you can compare it with one at the other end of the trail. Notice the tree overcome with mistletoe and the small, superthick grove of paloverde. Only 100 feet later, a stone bridge with cable handrails spans a wash, but it is not really a bridge, it is a dam for water control during a cloudburst. Next, pass through the picnic area and follow the arrow on a sign that indicates that the trail veers off to the left.

Stop before descending the first set of stairs and take a careful look at the large prickly pear cactus that most likely was partially

Petroglyphs

eaten by a hungry animal and not a starving picnicker. The trail then crosses a 15-foot-wide, very sandy wash before starting up the hill to the top. With the children, look at the green plants growing along the wash. More plants grow along washes because of the water channeled to their roots, yet the same water that nourishes also uproots. Ask the children whether they think the next rainstorm will bring more life, or take it away?

Just past the wash, a dead tree with twisted branches will take years to decompose in the dry desert environment. Halfway up the second set of stairs, the trail makes a 90-degree turn to the left, then almost immediately another 90-degree turn, this one to the right. Before the children walk around the first turn, have them take a step back and look at the stones that form the stairs. The face of one of the steps is made of a stone with a stunning, swirling pattern that only nature could make.

Now have them look to the left of the trail at the enormous compass cactus that is about 2 feet in diameter. It is significantly bigger than the cactus growing close to the trailhead—do they remember it?

Finish the short jaunt to the top, where black basalt rocks provide the medium for old petroglyph carvings made by the Hohokam Indians more than 600 years ago. What do the children think the spirals and other people-like figures could mean? There is no climbing permitted on the rocks, so contemplate from a distance.

After you have seen all there is to see, return along the same fun path.

40. Hunter Trail

Location: Picacho Peak State Park
Difficulty: Moderate to strenuous
Distance: 4 miles round trip
Hiking time: 4.5 hours
Hikable: October–May
Elevation gain: 1,574 feet
Map: USGS Newman Peak

Rising some 1,500 feet from its flat surroundings, Picacho Peak provides one of the more popular hikes in Arizona. The peak is the site of a Civil War battle and is along the route of the Mormon Battalion, which walked past Picacho Peak in 1846 when they marched from

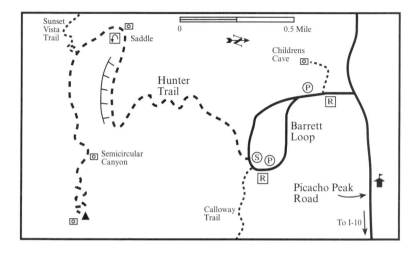

Council Bluffs, Iowa, to San Diego, California—the longest infantry march in U.S. history. Life seen along the way includes swifts and doves that live in holes in the cliffs, saguaro, cholla, paloverde, and ocotillo. Although there are several trails in Picacho Peak State Park, Hunter Trail is the only one that leads to the peak, and it is the most popular. However, it is not a hike suitable for little children; there are parts that are so steep that cable handrails were installed. But it is a great hike for older children, because the challenging terrain demands their complete attention. The park staff advises that children be at least ten years old. Even though it sounds like a hard hike, the first leg to the saddle between two peaks can be enjoyed by children of all ages. You need to have both hands free to do the hike, so use a backpack or a fanny pack to carry your water and other things. Bathrooms and water are located at the trailhead.

Driving Instructions: Picacho Peak State Park is southeast of Phoenix. Take Interstate 10 south toward Tucson. At exit 219, 70 miles from Phoenix, exit and follow the signs about 2 miles to the park entrance. From the park office, continue straight on Picacho Peak Road, then turn left on Barrett Loop. Follow the road around until you reach the parking area on the right that is closest to its adjacent rest rooms. There are signs for Calloway and Hunter Trails.

Note: The Children's Cave Trailhead is close to the other parking area and rest rooms. It is a very easy, 0.2-mile hike for little children. There is a bridge over a dry wash, and at the destination there are some tall rocks.

Cable handrails make a steep descent easier.

A neighboring peak as seen from Picacho Peak

From the trailhead, elevation 2,000 feet, Picacho Peak and the mountains on either side are tall and impressive. The ground slopes upward to the base of the large, sheer cliffs of the peak. As the trail winds its way from the trailhead toward the base of the cliff, it passes through a short, steep section that has handrails. Children of any age can make it with help from an adult.

At about 0.75 mile, the trail reaches the cliff and then follows it to the saddle. Erosion has carved pockets into the base of the cliff like round scoops out of ice cream; however, none of the holes are very big. Continue along the trail to the hike's halfway point at the saddle, where a bench provides rest and a few rocky areas offer more exploration. The hike to the saddle and back is a pleasant 2-mile round trip that is worth doing with small children.

From the saddle, the Hunter Trail descends sharply on the other side of the mountain. It is a steep, improved trail with hand cables for support. The Sunset Vista Trail intersects the Hunter Trail on the right 0.25 mile beyond the saddle; continue straight ahead to stay on the Hunter Trail. Where the descent ends, the trail begins an ascent so steep that it is more like climbing than hiking. It is a challenge for older children, but the handrails make it possible and safe. The steep trail continues with occasional level sections until it reaches a small, semicircular canyon at 1.6 miles. After the level canyon, there is only one more very steep, hard section before the last short, easy walk to the top.

Because the hike is popular, you probably will not have the peak to yourselves. The view from the top is superb. The closest mountains, the rest of the Picacho Mountain Range, lie to the north, just across Interstate 10. All others are far in the distance across a flat, seemingly endless expanse. If you take binoculars, you can see hundreds of ostriches on the farm next to the highway. Ask the children to try to imagine where the 1862 Civil War battle occurred, or take the hike in the spring when the battle is reenacted by people in authentic dress.

Relax before the return trip, then return to the trailhead by the same route.

41. Coronado Cave Trail

Location: Coronado National Memorial
Difficulty: Moderate
Distance: 1.5 miles round trip; 0.5 mile of caving
Hiking time: 2.25 hours
Hikable: Year-round
Elevation gain: 470 feet
Map: USGS Montezuma Pass

Where can you crawl through tunnels, witness the green, glowing eye and teeth of a "dinosaur," and see huge scallops on dry land? Only in Coronado Cave. Coronado Cave Trail leads to a live cave that you can explore without getting lost. The cave is well preserved, with beautiful stalactites, stalagmites, columns, scallops, and curtains. Because the cave is still growing, do not touch any of the formations or any cave creatures like crickets or bats you may encounter. Small children need help over the boulders in the entrance. One flashlight per person, including children, is required. Helmets are optional, but highly recommended. Take lots of water, but no food into the cave. You need a free permit from the Visitors Center to enter the cave.

Driving Instructions: From Tucson, travel east on Interstate 10 for 45 miles to the State Highway 90 intersection. Go south on State Highway 90 for 30 miles to its intersection with State Highway 92 in Sierra Vista. Follow Highway 92 south approximately 16 miles to Coronado Memorial Road, also known as Forest Road 61. Take a right onto the forest road and continue 2 miles south, where it curves sharply to the right and assumes the name East Montezuma Canyon Road. Continue on the road about 1 mile to the Coronado National Memorial Visitors Center on the right-hand side of the road. Park in the lot and go into the Visitors Center to get a free permit to explore the cave. The trailhead, elevation 5,230 feet, is at the west end of the parking lot just across a small road.

The wayside sign at the trailhead describes the cave's formation thousands of years ago as water dissolved the limestone, then flowed to lower elevations. The trail starts as an easy walk down through a wash, then up the other side. The first 0.2 mile is an easy stroll through manzanita, cane cholla with purple springtime blooms, and oaks and sycamores. Blue Mexican jays fly through the air, calling noisily to each other. Tell children to keep a special watch for deer because it is not uncommon to see them along the trail. Children can also look at the ground to see the large ants busy at work.

The moderate, continuous climb begins just past the utility shed on the left. With switchbacks and some shaded sections, the trail rises steadily for 0.5 mile. Oak trees along the way provided excellent acorns to inspect, while an occasional pine tree adds variety to the terrain. The trail ends right at the boulders in the cave's entrance. Stop to put on your helmets, then help small children over the boulders and down the sloping cave entrance to the level floor inside. The light flooding in from the entrance reveals a large chamber, but there is not enough light to make out any details.

Move ahead and to the right until the room narrows and the floor to the left leads up to a plateau. Look at the strangely shaped rocks and ask the children to imagine what they look like. It is not hard to find what looks like rats, turtles, and other animals in stony relief. Also look at the eerie formations on the wall to the right. Climb the incline to the left and walk to the wall. Small semicircular openings

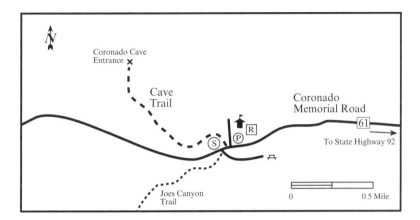

lead through the wall to a tunnel. Follow the tunnel deeper into the cave until it stops. Look at the scallops that grow from the wall and float out overhead in addition to every bump on the ceiling that someday may grow into a stalactite. Remind children not to touch anything, or the oils on their fingers may stop the formations from growing.

Leave the tunnel through one of its many semicircular openings and cross a pile of boulders to the right side of the cave. Scan the roof occasionally to see if there are any bats hanging high above or any interesting stalactites. Walk down the right side of the cave a few feet to a fork in the path. The left path leads up deeper into the main chamber; the right leads downward into a small opening. Crawl through this opening into a small 3-foot-diameter tunnel.

As you crawl down the tunnel, an intersection appears after 10 feet. The branch to the right leads to an opening just over 1 foot in diameter. Stay straight in the larger tunnel. As you crawl along, look at the tiny formations all along the roof. After about 30 feet, the tunnel turns to reveal that it continues another 20 feet, after which there is another curve, 20 more feet, and then a dead end. Children find it exciting to crawl single-file through such bizarre surroundings. Watch for light-colored cave crickets along the way.

Return from the tunnel and this time at the fork, take the left path, which leads to the narrow passage between the front and back caverns. Look back to see light filtering in from the entrance and the mysterious, space-age formations hanging from the ceiling. As the cave narrows, walk along a wall of stone on the right, which does not reach to the ceiling. On top of the wall are the legs, back, and finally at the end of the wall, the head of a stone dinosaur. Its nose points down to the ground with teeth in its open mouth, two ears, and one eye. Have everyone shine their lights on the dinosaur's eye and stare at it hard. Then, at the very same moment, have everyone switch their lights off. As you continue to stare in the dark, the eye and the teeth glow a strange green color.

Just past the dinosaur is the smaller back chamber where a small, rocky tunnel off the right side leads to three short tunnels that are difficult to enter. At the back of the chamber, where the floor rises up, a beautiful column connects the floor and ceiling. The texture of the column's ribs are curved by the water that deposited the calcium from the limestone. To the left of the column is an opening that leads to a small back room. Light filters down from the back entrance high above a pile of boulders.

The back entrance is closed, so return through the front entrance. Once you exit the cave, return back down the path.

42. Coronado Peak Trail

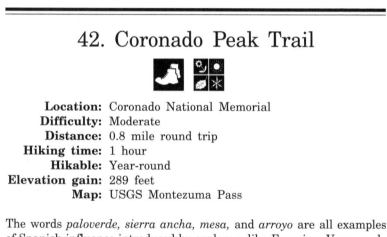

Location: Coronado National Memorial
Difficulty: Moderate
Distance: 0.8 mile round trip
Hiking time: 1 hour
Hikable: Year-round
Elevation gain: 289 feet
Map: USGS Montezuma Pass

The words *paloverde, sierra ancha, mesa,* and *arroyo* are all examples of Spanish influence introduced by explorers like Francisco Vasquez de Coronado. The short Coronado Peak Trail commemorates that Spaniard's arrival in Arizona, in 1540 A.D., during his two-year quest for cities filled with gold, known as the Seven Cities of Cibola. The moderate ascent is broken by rest breaks to read the plaques along the trail that recount the group's journey and hardships. Close your eyes and you can almost see the dusty specters of conquistadors on their trek just as they were more than 450 years ago. In the spring, blossoms on small bushes and wildflowers add color along the way to the peak. From the top, the green stripe of trees along the San Pedro River cuts across the wide valley far below. Birds soar over nearby Montezuma Peak, and the pointed tip of San Jose Peak is visible just south of the border in Mexico. There are bathrooms at the south end of the parking lot. The water at the covered picnic shelter is available only during the summer and is not reliable, so take all the water you will need.

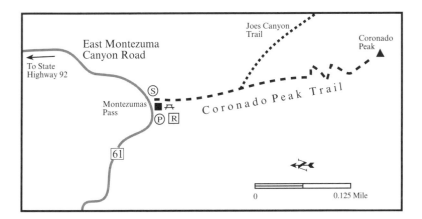

Driving Instructions: From Tucson, travel east on Interstate 10 for 45 miles to its intersection with State Highway 90. Go south on Highway 90, through Sierra Vista. At the intersection with State Highway 92, turn right onto Highway 92 and travel south approximately 16 miles to Coronado Memorial Road, also known as Forest Road 61, on the right. Take the road 2 miles south, where it curves sharply to the right and assumes the name East Montezuma Canyon Road. Continue on about 1 mile to the Coronado National Memorial Visitors Center. About 1 mile past the Visitors Center, the road becomes dirt. Continue for 2 miles as it climbs up the valley to the area labeled Montezumas Pass. At the pass, turn left into the large parking area. The trailhead, elevation 6,575 feet, is behind the sheltered picnic area.

The trail immediately starts a moderate ascent and after 0.1 mile intersects with Joes Canyon Trail on the left. Continue straight on Coronado Peak Trail. The sotol plant along the trail was given the name *cuchara*, or "spoon," by the Spaniards because when a dried leaf is pulled from the plant, its end looks like a spoon. The beargrass is also known as basket grass to Mexicans, who still use it to make baskets.

Nine plaques, each about 200 feet apart, lead to the peak and recount some aspect of Coronado's 1540–1542 journey recorded in journals. The showy start of the journey, with elaborate uniforms and ostentatious farewell ceremonies, is recorded on the first plaque, while the others detail the ensuing fatigue, thirst, hunger, and impassable mountains as the journey proceeded. Their journals reveal that their purpose was considered a missionary expedition in addition to finding great wealth and claiming possession of land for Spain.

Coronado's journey was considered a failure because they did not return with fantastic wealth, but fifty-four years later, in 1596, one member of the group reminisced that the value of the journey was in discovering a new land. Gold was the lure, but the real prize was the bountiful land the Spaniards soon began to settle. They brought with them names and customs that are still with us today.

The benches at the plaques provide the opportunity to sit while enjoying the purple blossoms of the cane cholla in the spring, which occasionally houses the nest of a cactus wren in its thorny branches. The peaceful silence of the desert permeates the entire region. Small bushes dot the mountain and sway in the breeze. Little has changed since its first discovery by Europeans. Follow the trail and the unfolding saga of Coronado's trip to the top of the mountain where the view opens to a narrow valley that leads to a large, flat plain. The thin ribbon of green shows the San Pedro River's course across the plain and also the travelers' route so long ago. Turkey vultures soar over Montezumas Peak to the left just as they did hundreds of years ago.

Enriched by the beauty of the desert and knowledge of a part of its history, return from the peak along the same trail.

---

43. Echo Canyon and Hailstone Trails

Location: Chiricahua National Monument
Difficulty: Moderate
Distance: 3.5-mile loop
Hiking time: 3 hours
Hikable: May-October
Elevation gain: 450 feet
Map: USGS Cochise Head

Tall, very flat walls of stone that form the corridor known as Wall Street, spherulites, and massive boulders balanced on 300-foot stone columns are only some of the phenomenal natural formations in the strange, unique land of the Chiricahua Mountains. The trail descends from scrub, windblown trees to magnificent pine giants in an area known as Echo Park, and winds through towering pillars with purple and green hues carved thousands of years ago by wind and water. Closely spaced, massive columns form a labyrinth of hallways between their bases. The well-constructed trail uses switchbacks to make the trail enjoyable even for young children.

Driving Instructions: From Tucson, travel 76 miles east on

A unique cluster of stone spires along Echo Canyon Trail

Interstate 10 to the city of Willcox. From Willcox, follow State Highway 186 south 26 miles to State Highway 181. Turn left (east) on Highway 181 and travel about 3 miles to the entrance to Chiricahua National Monument. Continue straight past the entrance as the road becomes Bonita Canyon Drive. Drive approximately 7.5 miles to a turnoff marked with signs for "ECHO CANYON AND SUGARLOAF" parking. Turn right onto this road, and travel approximately 0.5 mile to the Echo Canyon parking lot turnoff on the left. The trailhead is at the end of the lot, elevation 6,780 feet.

The wide, well-defined trail starts in surroundings of beargrass, manzanita, small scrub bushes, and stunted trees, and proceeds to the first of many balancing rocks, 150 feet from the trailhead. This formation looks like a bird perched on a pillar with its head pointing to the right. At the intersection 150 feet past the bird, stay to the right to head down into Echo Canyon.

Point out to children that the rocks of the area have different shades that hint about their formation. Twenty-seven million years ago, the Turkey Creek Caldera volcano covered the entire area with a 2,000-foot-thick blanket of ash, which fused together to form welded tuff that ranges from very soft to completely welded, hard stone. Tuff of the same hardness does not all occur on the same level, so uplift and cracking, combined with wind and water erosion, formed stones of strange, nonuniform shapes. Wind carves the balancing rocks by eating away the soft tuff around a column, leaving the hard stone resting on a narrow base at the top.

At 0.2 mile, the trail narrows and descends past a pile of boulders that look like they were stacked on top of each other, but in reality the entire pile was once a single stone that eroded unevenly to leave what looks like separate boulders. To the left of the trail, the rocks

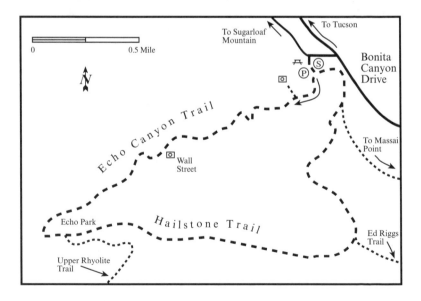

stacked against each other look like toy blocks, while another rock balances about 15 feet over the trail. Encourage children to touch the rock's rough texture and look closely at the fluorescent green lichens that cover and almost hide the natural brown and purplish hues. Other balancing rocks stand near the trail, and the distant valley below is covered with narrow-looking, greenish pillars.

At 0.3 mile, pass between the two 25-foot pillars to a turnoff to the right of the trail that leads to a massive balancing rock the size of two or three buses; it must weigh several tons.

As the trail descends, there are even more columns with diameters of between 20 and 40 feet, but even more intriguing are the nooks and passages between the closely spaced spires that wind and twist before disappearing out of sight. At 0.45 mile, stones fallen from their pedestals above form a mixed-up pile. One rock crashed into a pine tree, which survived and grows around the boulder's jagged edge. Where the trail makes a sharp 270-degree turn to the left, at 0.65 mile, look for two columns, one of which has fallen over and leans against the other.

The trail descends around and between columns until at 0.9 mile it is flanked on both sides by the tall, very flat walls that form the corridor known as Wall Street. The flat walls seem out of place in an area dominated by rounded pillars and highly eroded, rough rocks. Turn around at the end of Wall Street to see a balancing rock perfectly framed by the wall's straight lines.

The trees grow taller as the trail descends to the thick forest of Echo Park at 1.2 miles, where columns can be seen only through breaks in the trees. A dry creekbed, with occasional pools of water, cuts through the park, and big stones, the remnants of pillars, lie between the trees. By 1.45 miles, the lush forest ends and the trail starts an ascent over hot slopes where the trees are once again stunted from exposure. A sign at 1.6 miles marks the intersection of Echo Canyon Trail with Hailstone Trail and Upper Rhyolite Trail. Take the left fork to proceed along the Hailstone Trail.

The dry terrain supports desert plants like alligator juniper, prickly pear cacti, and numerous century plants. Have children look carefully along the trail for mounds of dirt where minuscule brown ants struggle to remove miniature grains of sand from their nest entrance. The stone pillars above the trail are seen from a new perspective, and in several places, balancing rocks have tipped off their bases and wedged between columns.

Small, white, spherical stones, called spherulites, are usually found in clumps with many stuck together, but occasionally loose ones are found. Once the volcanic ash landed on the ground, the spherulites formed in place through a process that is similar to crystallization, and they are found throughout the Chiricahua area. The large clumps

A fallen pillar rests against its neighbor.

of spherulites at 2 miles look like models of molecules from a science lab. It was once believed that these rocks formed like hailstones in clouds of volcanic ash, but recent research showed that they did not form in the air, but on the ground.

The trail ascends along a deep canyon studded with columns and occasionally shaded by trees until an intersection at 2.25 miles with the Ed Riggs Trail on the right. Take the left fork to continue on Hailstone Trail, and by the 2.3-mile point, columns once more stand next to the trail, inviting children to inspect their scaly, rough surfaces.

Big boulders abound, but the tall columns are less frequent as the trail continues its slight ascent through tall pines and wavyleaf oak undergrowth. At 2.8 miles the trail makes a 270-degree right turn across the dry drainage that parallels the trail and is the resting place of many massive boulders. At the intersection at 2.9 miles, take the left fork (the right leads to Massai Point), then at the intersection at 3.2 miles take the right fork as signs point the way back to the parking lot. Near the end, plants are once again stunted and wind-blown, while the massive columns, strange formations, and tall pines are obscured.

44. Sugarloaf Mountain Trail

Location: Chiricahua National Monument
Difficulty: Moderate
Distance: 1.8 miles round trip
Hiking time: 1.5 hours
Hikable: May-October
Elevation gain: 470 feet
Map: USGS Cochise Head

What appears to be an average trail climbs to uncommon views, but not before passing tiny plants growing in minuscule holes in rocks, plus a tunnel, a picnic table made of stone slabs, a manzanita thicket, and hundreds of white footprints. The hard lava rock seen along the ascent protected the hill from the erosion that turned the soft tuff of the area into deep canyons. The summit houses a fire lookout station and offers unbroken views of tall stone pillars that stand as silent sentinels in the valleys below, every bit as intriguing as the massive heads that guard Easter Island. There is no bathroom or water at the trailhead; carry all the water you will need.

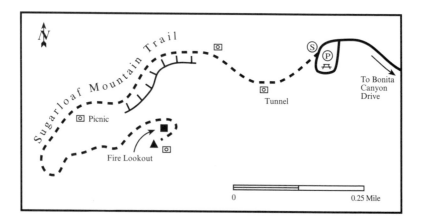

Driving Instructions: From Tucson, travel 76 miles east on Interstate 10 to the city of Willcox. From Willcox, follow State Highway 186 south for 26 miles to State Highway 181. Turn left (east) on Highway 181 and travel about 3 miles to the entrance to Chiricahua National Monument. Continue straight past the entrance as the road becomes Bonita Canyon Drive. Drive approximately 7.5 miles to a turnoff marked with signs for "ECHO CANYON AND SUGARLOAF" parking. Turn right on the road and travel to its terminus, which is marked as the parking lot for Sugarloaf Mountain. The trailhead is at the end of the lot, elevation 6,840 feet.

Cut into the side of the mountain, the well-maintained dirt trail starts an immediate ascent past ubiquitous pinyon pine, manzanita, and alligator junipers scattered between brown and rust-colored rocks. A 5-foot-tall stone escarpment flanks the left side of the trail, while the right opens to a valley of distant, stone columns.

Have the children look into the tiny holes eroded into the rock along the trail where even smaller plants miraculously take root in a valiant effort to grow. How do the tiny roots get water and nutrients through solid stone? How did the tiny seeds get into the holes? Rainwater either falls directly into the holes or it seeps through the porous rock into the holes. The plant seeds are usually carried by wind, but they can also be transported by ants. Plants do not grow in every hollow, so encourage the children to search carefully. Grasses cover the hillside along with large clumps of beargrass and pretty purple wildflowers.

The tunnel at 0.15 mile was cut through solid stone by the Civilian Conservation Corps when the trail was built in the 1935. Just 250 feet past the tunnel, a cavity eroded in a natural stone column has two pieces of rock hanging from the top like teeth in an open mouth.

More of the valley is seen below, along with a broad plain beyond the mountains in the distance.

Near the 0.3-mile mark, a cliff of white rock capped by rust-colored stone begins to appear. The white rock is very soft, volcanic tuff, while the red is the hard lava layer that protected the hill from erosion. After an ancient volcanic eruption covered the entire area with a thick layer of ash that fused together to become volcanic tuff, a layer of volcanic dacite from the caldera covered a small section. Over millions of years, erosion cut away at the tuff but could not get through the hard dacite, thereby leaving Sugarloaf Mountain as the highest point in the local area.

As the trail continues uphill, the white cliff to the side gets taller, but it is always capped with the red lava. At 0.35 mile, part of the lava broke from the top and left a jumble of large rocks behind some bushes. Near the 0.4-mile point, sections of the white rock show black, exposed lines that give the stone the appearance of marble. As the cliffs continue, the trail becomes covered with a white dust from the

A short break at a picnic table of natural stone

stone. Children can touch the stone to see the white, chalk-like dust left on their finger, and look at all of the footsteps recorded in fine powder on the ground.

At 0.5 mile, by the side of the cliff a small picnic table made from slabs of natural stone invites passersby to rest and possibly eat lunch. The elevation provides views of a long valley below filled with narrow columns of a green hue. The way the spires rise above their surroundings and dot the land is reminiscent of the huge stone heads that poke out of the grasses on Easter Island. The huge boulders balanced atop the columns are like the topknots that once graced the heads of Easter Island before they fell off. The columns of the silent valley look as though they are patiently waiting for some unknown event to happen.

The curve in the trail at 0.6 mile reveals a new valley, called the Heart of Rocks, that is also filled with pillars of rock colored green. Manzanita grows more abundantly along the trail, along with junipers and small pinyon pines, but by 0.7 mile the manzanita chokes out all other plants. Like a 4-foot-tall hedge, the branches of separate bushes intertwine into a red thicket so dense it is impossible to see through it.

By 0.85 mile, the trail passes the fire lookout station on the summit and ends 250 feet later at a spectacular lookout over the unique valley of stone columns. As you pass the fire lookout, notice the protection against lightning strikes: thick copper wires that encompass the building before disappearing into the ground.

After enjoying the view and reading the signs that tell about the area, return by the same route.

45. Massai Point Nature Trail

Location: Chiricahua National Monument
Difficulty: Easy
Distance: 0.5-mile loop
Hiking time: 0.5 hour
Hikable: May–October
Elevation gain: 270 feet
Map: USGS Cochise Head

The Massai Point Nature Trail, easy even for small children, offers all of the wonders of the Chiricahua Mountains: stone columns, balancing

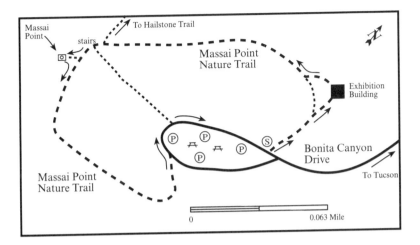

rocks, winding trails, and even a fortress-like viewpoint. Beargrass, stunted pinyon pines, gnarled alligator juniper, yucca, and manzanita grow between unique, highly eroded stone formations that are close-up and accessible to children. The Exhibition Building near the trailhead is a must-see. Constructed of welded volcanic tuff from the area, it houses a huge relief map, wooden models of stone columns, spheru-lites, and pictures of the more famous balancing rocks. The Chiricahua Mountains are enchanting, intriguing, and unique. Once covered by a thick layer of welded tuff, which is volcanic ash that is fused together, uplift and erosion transformed the area into valleys filled with tall, mysterious pillars of solid stone with even more spectacular boulders precariously balanced atop many of the columns. This trail is a short but complete introduction to the Chiricahua National Monument. There are neither bathrooms nor water at the trailhead.

Driving Instructions: From Tucson travel 76 miles east on Inter-state 10 to the city of Willcox. From Willcox, follow State Highway 186 south 26 miles to State Highway 181. Turn left (east) on Highway 181 and travel about 3 miles to the park entrance. Continue straight past the entrance as the road becomes Bonita Canyon Drive. Stay on the road until it ends in a loop in about 9 miles. The trailhead, elevation 6,870 feet, is on the right near the entrance to the loop.

The trail starts on the right side of the loop road, where a sign marks the Massai Point Nature Trail. At the intersection just 50 feet after the trailhead, stay to the right to go directly to the Exhibition Building. There are other intersections along the way, but the building is in view at the top of a small rise.

Inside, the mysteries of the Chiricahua formations are revealed.

A huge relief map shows the surrounding mountains and the various trails. Displays, carved of wood, show how the solid layer of volcanic tuff slowly transformed along joints and faults to be free-standing pillars and balanced rocks. Signs explain how tuff varies from the lightly welded, soft, and easily eroded to the completely welded, hard, erosion-resistant stone. Spherulites, round stones formed from volcanic ash through a form of crystallization, are displayed and explained. Pictures of the most famous balancing rocks on some of the longer trails are also shown. The building itself contains the final lesson about the area because it is made completely of welded tuff of various degrees of hardness, and provides a format for easy comparison. Walk around the back of the building, looking at the tuff, to the sign labeled "ALL TRAILS."

Signs continue to point the way as the mostly dirt trail passes over sections of solid stone, past windblown, twisted trees and nature signs to a stone pillar at 0.2 mile. The 12-foot column is an up-close, miniature version of the huge spires that tower in the valley below. With the children, look closely at the green and black lichens on the rocks. The green lichens are the most prolific and give the rocks in the area a greenish color. More balanced rocks come into view, and explanatory displays of their formation stand close to the trail.

Look for rocks where erosion narrowed the base more than the upper portions. A balancing rock forms when the wind removes the soft tuff between two sections of hard tuff. The rock stays balanced on its narrow base until the day when it erodes too much, then it topples from its perch to the ground. Mixed in with the formations are yucca, manzanita, beargrass, pinyon pine, and alligator juniper, but the plant life is not abundant.

The formation at 0.25 mile is a close-up, excellent example of a balancing rock. Just past the rock, an intersection that leads to the Hailstone Trail, to the right, has a sign that indicates that the nature trail continues to the left and leads to more balancing rocks, where children can walk entirely around them to see all sides. At another intersection almost immediately after, the left fork is a shortcut back to the parking area; take the right fork as it leads down a set of stairs, and then a short spur trail to the right takes you to Massai Point: a round, fortress-like lookout that provides a fascinating view of the hundreds of columns in the deep valley below.

Descend from the lookout and go to the right to regain the nature trail. At 0.35 mile, the trail passes between two boulders about 12 feet apart and gives small children the flavor of passing between the tall towers seen from Massai Point. The next formation is a dramatic balancing rock where the base's diameter is much smaller than the rock perched on top: a perfect example of how erosion leaves leviathans balanced on relatively tiny spires.

The dirt trail ends 150 feet later as it emerges onto the loop road. You could return immediately to your car, but good views and explanatory signs are posted along the loop, so stay to the left and follow the edge of the asphalt. At 0.45 mile a sign on the left shows the short path from the parking lot down to the Massai Point lookout. The trailhead is only an additional 150 feet straight ahead, and ends this perfect introductory loop through a strange, wonderful land.

46. Dutch John Spring Trail

Location: Madera Canyon, Santa Rita Mountains
Difficulty: Moderate
Distance: 3.6 miles round trip
Hiking time: 3 hours
Hikable: Year-round
Elevation gain: 200 feet
Map: USGS Mt. Wrightson

The trees along the Dutch John Spring Trail not only provide shade, but they are also sanctuary to hundreds of different types of birds that make Madera Canyon an internationally known birding area. Take a bird identification book and put names to the birds in view. In addition to the wildlife, there are strangely shaped Arizona sycamores, two springs, and red-colored rocks. Leaves from dense oak thickets litter the ground and rustle underfoot. Be on the lookout for beautiful thistles in bloom, yellow wildflowers, and giant alligator junipers. Purify the water from the springs before drinking, or carry all you will need for the hike.

Driving Instructions: On Interstate 19, south of Tucson, take exit 63 eastbound. Turn east onto Continental Road, then turn right onto White House Canyon Road. Stay on the paved road about 12 miles until the left turn to Bog Spring Campground. Follow the loop through the campground almost all the way around to a parking area where there are spaces set aside for hikers. There is a parking fee. From the parking area, cross the road, ascend the short flight of stone steps, and follow the well-worn path to the sign that marks the trailhead, elevation 4,820 feet.

A short 100 feet past the sign, a V gate through the fence limits traffic to pedestrians. Big boulders, some with a dark red hue, lie in

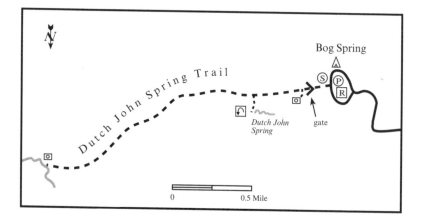

a dry creekbed 40 feet below the trail. At the intersection 100 feet past the gate, the left fork leads up a short hill to views of tall mountains and a thick forest of oak trees that cover the valley leading to the springs. The leaves of the Arizona sycamores turn golden in the fall and provide dashes of color along the dry creekbeds. Take the left fork if you wish to see the view, then return to the main trail and turn left to continue the hike; to skip the overlook, at the intersection follow the right fork.

Try to identify any of the scores of beautiful birds as they chirp and flutter in the trees overhead. A strange sycamore grows next to the trail at 0.1 mile, just after the trail crosses the creekbed. Its main trunk grows horizontal to the ground and insects have eaten the internal wood until it looks like lace, yet in spite of the trunk's condition, healthy branches sprout from it and grow skyward. Have the children watch for red and purple rocks along the way and wherever the trail crosses a drainage. The trees are so thick in areas that moss grows on many of them; piles of dried leaves on the trail rustle with each step. The steady climb is broken momentarily at 0.3 mile where a brown fiberglass sign marks the Mount Wrightson Wilderness Area boundary. Children can keep a lookout along the drainage for sycamores whose trunks are strangely formed.

The upward climb continues to an almost imperceivable intersection at 0.35 mile, where the left fork descends to a sign that marks the small metal tank as being Dutch John Spring. The moisture from the spring supports yellow wildflowers and a host of thistles. Mushrooms grow in a hollow stump, a huge log makes a great bench for a short rest, and another strangely shaped sycamore allows close inspection.

Enjoy the spring, then continue up the main trail to where it flattens out at 0.4 mile as it crosses the wide, dry creek again and then climbs out of the bed past a distinct group of four large sycamores. The trail narrows as it cuts through terrain covered with large clumps of beargrass until at 0.45 mile it arrives at a false intersection where the trail appears to continue straight into the creekbed, but in reality it turns 270 degrees to the right. Watch for the rock cairn that marks the path. Have the children look closely for bird feathers; they are not hard to find.

Boulders appear among the trees, while occasional golden penstemon flowers add color to the wavyleaf oaks that crowd the trail. Acorn caps and thick leaves litter the ground. At 0.55 mile, to the right of the trail there is an old oak tree that was burnt by fire, yet somehow managed to live. The growth around the burn left it twisted and with a weird shape. A bit further up, a 4-foot-long stump covers half the trail, which descends again into the creekbed. On the other side, the trail passes a small concrete tank that once collected springwater and ends near a natural pool fed by water from the hill behind it. The water nourishes abundant trees, thick grasses, yucca, moss, and prickly pear cacti.

Once again, enjoy the lush environment supported by the spring, then return along the same route.

Spring water storage tank

47. Madera Canyon Nature Trail

Location: Madera Canyon, Santa Rita Mountains
Difficulty: Easy
Distance: 2.7 miles round trip
Hiking time: 2 hours
Hikable: Year-round
Elevation gain: 510 feet
Maps: USGS Mt. Wrightson, USGS Mt. Hopkins

The open, mostly level Madera Canyon Nature Trail crosses a creek over a wooden bridge, then climbs slightly to panoramic views of the Santa Rita Mountains and soaring Mount Wrightson. Large outcroppings of weathered granite and rose-colored rocks add texture to the terrain, while tiny, single-sprig ferns hide in the undergrowth waiting to be found by alert children. Signs along the way point out mountain muly grass and resurrection plant, and explain geotropism. Much of the trail is open, providing little shade during the summer. Hiking just the first 0.4 mile of the trail makes it perfect for small children. There are no bathrooms or water at the trailhead.

Driving Instructions: On Interstate 19 south of Tucson, take exit 63 eastbound. Turn east on Continental Road, then turn right onto White House Canyon Road. Stay on the paved road about 13 miles to the signs that mark the Amphitheater and Nature Trail. Turn right into the parking area. The trailhead is at the back of the lot, elevation 4,630 feet.

Note: The Madera Canyon Nature Trail stretches from the parking area near the Amphitheater to the Roundup Picnic Area at the road's end. To return to your car, you must either return along the entire trail or walk down the road. Because the road can be very busy at times, the hike described here stays on the trail.

Follow the paved trail from the parking lot down to a wooden bridge that crosses a stony creekbed. Water flows down the creek in the spring, if winter weather left snow in the crags of the high Santa Rita Mountains, and for about an hour after a rainstorm, but most of the time the bed is dry; however, enough water flows to support sycamore trees like the strangely shaped one at the end of the bridge.

At the intersection just past the bridge, take the left fork where the trail changes from asphalt to dirt and passes behind the small amphitheater. Almost immediately, the trail starts a slight ascent through a rocky section where solid granite rock decomposes into wheat-sized grains. Tiny ferns, between 1 and 2 inches high, grow out of the ground as a single branch instead of a clump of branches. Small oak trees grow near rocks colored red by iron oxide (rust). Four hundred feet from the bridge, resurrection plants grow abundantly on the hillside, holding the topsoil in place.

When the trail was cut into the hillside, the roots of many trees were left exposed as a perfect cross section of how roots sink into the ground, even growing around rocks to get past them to water. Have the children look carefully at the length of the roots to see that as much of the tree grows below ground as above. A huge rock over-hangs the trail at 0.1 mile where a sign marks the hollow opening at its base as an animal cave. A quick succession of signs identify mountain muly, a grass that likes granitic soils; granite, an intrusive volcanic rock; and geotropism, when things grow downward toward the force of gravity. Berries from junipers, some up to ¼ inch in diameter, and decomposing granitic rock from large outcroppings, litter the well-maintained trail.

A large sign and picture at 0.4 mile identify the locations and names of the mountains of the entire Santa Rita range that lies in panoramic splendor directly ahead. The nearby bench provides rest while you drink in the deep green of the lower altitudes and the dull gray of Mount Wrightson's rocky heights. More pines appear as the trail cuts across the deep, valley-like drainages that carry water from the hilltops to the valley floors. See if the children can watch carefully for manzanita bushes, and find the first one along the trail.

The water in the drainage at 0.6 mile supports lush grasses and wildflowers, while the same water leaves twisted furrows in the barren hills of predominantly granitic soil. Some granite outcroppings have a rosy hue reminiscent of a beautiful sunset. The dark green stones

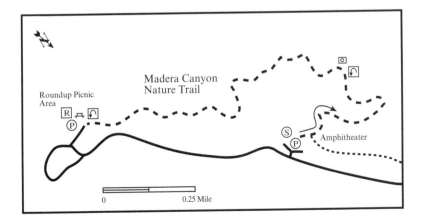

occasionally found along the trail are not jade, but are just as interesting in an area of so much gray granite. A huge, dead tree 25 to 30 feet tall stands at the 0.85-mile point, while a bench provides a rest spot at 0.95 mile. Beyond the bench, the undergrowth is thick, and apache pines with their pom-poms of 6-inch-long needles at the ends of their branches become more common.

At 1.1 miles, the trail turns into a 2-foot-wide strip of concrete that curves through thick oaks splotched with moss, then at 1.2 miles it goes around a fence corner and enters private land. Permission to pass has been granted by the owner, so show respect by staying on the concrete path. The trail parallels the creek for 500 feet, then crosses its dry bed before climbing up to the end at the Roundup Picnic Area.

Enjoy a rest stop at the picnic area before returning to your car along the same route.

48. Red Tanks Tinaja Trail

Location: Organ Pipe Cactus National Monument
Difficulty: Easy
Distance: 1.3 miles round trip
Hiking time: 1 hour
Hikable: October-April
Elevation loss: 110 feet
Map: USGS Lukeville

A step into the past, the short hike to Red Tanks Tinaja is a reminder of the importance of water in the desert. Accompanied by large bushes of silver cholla, saguaro, ocotillo, creosote, and organ pipe cactus, the trail leads to a stone depression in a wash, called a *tinaja*, which means "bowl" or "tub" in Spanish. Today, as in ancient times, the tinaja holds water long after the rush from a rainstorm is gone. Unlike today, water in the tinaja preserved the lives of early desert travelers whose paths were constrained to follow the series of tinajas that lie in the washes winding through the desert. At the tinaja, children can look for water, bird feathers, and dried red mud from turbid waters. The easy trail is suitable for children of all ages. There are no bathrooms or water at the trailhead. Carry all the water you will need.

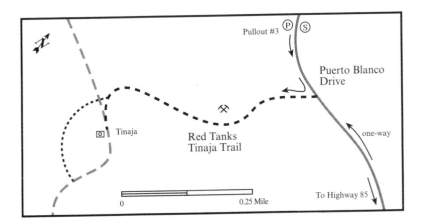

Driving Instructions: From Phoenix, travel south on Interstate 10 for 31 miles to the interchange with Interstate 8. Travel west on Interstate 8 for 65 miles to State Highway 85, then proceed 66 miles south on Highway 85, past the city of Why, to the well-marked pullout for the entrance to Organ Pipe Cactus National Monument. Pay the entrance fee at the small shack, then, from the Visitors Center, follow the signs that lead about 1 mile to the beginning of Puerto Blanco Drive. The entire loop through the park is over this 51-mile-long dirt road, and much of it is limited to one-way traffic. **Note:** There are no services along the way, so be sure that the car has enough gas to make the entire loop. From the start of Puerto Blanco Drive, travel 5 miles to pullout #3, which is a marked, wide spot in the road, elevation 1,840 feet, where you can park your car.

From the pullout, walk back on the road 0.2 mile to the sign for Red Tanks Tinaja primitive trail. Saguaro, sagebrush, and cholla dot the landscape. Have children look at the pleated folds in the saguaro. Are they deep from lack of rainfall, or has access to water made the cacti plump and the furrows shallow? Along the trail, notice the size of the silver cholla that range from 3 feet high with few joints to stately plants 4 to 5 feet high and about the same in diameter. The sun reflecting from their silver needles produces a bright halo around its branches.

At 0.25 mile, the trail passes through a sandy wash where piles of debris, snagged on bushes, accumulate. As the trail rises out of the wash, look at the nearby 40-foot saguaro. Step back for a more distant perspective that reveals its strange proportions. Its arms sprout from its body at a height of only 12 feet, giving it a strange, stunted look. Just above the arms, facing the trail, is a hole drilled by a gila woodpecker; there are several others on the other side of the cactus.

Organ Pipe National Monument

At 0.3 mile, 200 feet to the right of the trail a square fence surrounds an abandoned mine shaft. Dirt and a metal grating choke the entrance and the signs on the face say "DANGER—OPEN SHAFT." Small piles of greenish rock near the opening are the waste products of the old malachite mining operation. The almost round rock buried in the middle of the trail at 0.35 mile seems out of place because it is red, but it is the same color as the berries growing on the mistletoe that seems to plague most of the paloverde.

Along the sandy parts of the trail, have the children search for the conical depressions made by ant lions to trap ants to eat. Numerous young saguaro grow up next to their nurse plants and are shaped like upside-down bowling pins, their bases much smaller than their tops. Much of the way, the trail is a wide jeep or wagon track. Continue past sagebrush, organ pipe cactus, prickly pear cactus, and Mormon tea as the trail goes through a series of shallow washes. Notice the many groups of plants where saguaro, organ pipe cactus, paloverde, and silver cholla crowd together in a bunch separated from other nearby plants.

Rough, brown rock lies embedded in the packed dirt trail at 0.6 mile. Children can touch its weathered surface and see how its layers erode. The colors make it look more like wood than stone. Only a close inspection by touch detects its true nature, and even then it could almost pass as petrified wood. Only 250 feet later, at 0.65 mile, the trail appears to cross a wide, sandy wash, but a rock cairn leads to the left, down the wash a few hundred feet to the reddish, solid stone that forms the tinaja.

Descend into the tinaja and have the children look for water in its multitude of depressions. If there is no water, is the stone or shallow soil on top of the solid rock moist? Do feathers, left by thirsty birds, litter the ground? Continue down the wash over the stone about 40 feet to explore another arm of the tinaja to the left. Look at the red dirt deposited on the sides of the second arm by dirty water as it rushed through. The exposed roots of the mesquite tree are also painted red. Go almost to the end of the second arm, where on the left a small saguaro grows out of a solid stone. There are no other saguaro cacti nearby. How did the saguaro seed get to the tinaja? Was it carried by water or possibly by a bird?

As you leave the tinaja to return, look around at what represented life to the ancient traveler during a trip through the desert. Step out of the tinaja and return along the same path.

49. Dripping Springs Mine Trail

Location:	Organ Pipe Cactus National Monument
Difficulty:	Easy
Distance:	3.2 miles round trip
Hiking time:	3 hours
Hikable:	October–April
Elevation gain:	80 feet
Map:	USGS Kino Peak

Flanked by a sheer, tall cliff and rough, volcanic mountains, the Dripping Springs Mine Trail leads to a veritable forest of organ pipe cacti whose long, slender arms erupt from a common root and range

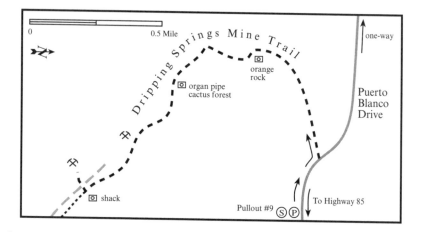

from tiny to huge. Be on the lookout for the dead remains of organ pipe, saguaro, and cholla cacti to compare their underlying skeletons. Orange and red rocks, stuck together by a white, cement-like stone, plus brown sand and birds' nests all wait to be discovered along the trek to two old, abandoned mines and piles of green tailings. The trail is suitable for children of all ages. There are neither bathrooms nor water at the trailhead.

Driving Instructions: From Phoenix, travel south on Interstate 10 for 31 miles to the interchange with Interstate 8. Travel west on Interstate 8 for 65 miles to State Highway 85, then proceed 66 miles south on Highway 85, past the city of Why, to the well-marked pullout for the entrance to Organ Pipe Cactus National Monument. Pay the entrance fee, then, continuing from the Visitors Center, follow the signs that lead about 1 mile to the beginning of Puerto Blanco Drive. The entire loop through the park is over this 51-mile-long dirt road, and much of it is limited to one-way traffic. **Note:** There are no services along the way, so be sure that the car has enough gas to make the entire loop. From the start of Puerto Blanco Drive, drive to pullout #9, elevation 1,860 feet, which is well-marked. Park your car and continue on foot in the same direction along the road 0.25 mile toward the trailhead.

The road and, subsequently, the trail pass a tall mountain on the left with a sheer 500-foot-cliff from which massive boulders have broken off and rolled into the valley below. Other nearby mountains are rough products of long-dead volcanoes. Organ pipe cacti dot their rugged slopes. The trailhead for the well-defined, earth-packed path is marked by a sign. The next 0.25 mile crosses several shallow washes and a thin covering of typical plant life: paloverde, Mormon tea, cholla, ocotillo, and sparse clumps of grass.

At 0.5 mile, just as the trail climbs out of another wash, look for orange-colored rocks with a texture that looks like pumice. The next wash has red and white stones at its bottom and, just beyond, an enormous, 12-foot-tall organ pipe cactus that has at least twenty arms. Have the children look closely at its regularly spaced clumps of straight, sharp needles. Although the slender arms sway in a breeze, they must be strong because none are broken off. The next wash contains even more red and orange rock. Compare the colors to the browns and whites commonly seen in the outdoors. How do the children suppose the orange rock was formed? Did it start as red rock, but somehow get mixed with a lighter-colored material before it cooled?

The dead saguaro at 0.75 mile, is unique. It appears to have tipped over, not at the roots, but 5 feet off the ground. It now looks

A sealed mine shaft

as though it is bowing. A short 0.1 mile later, conglomerate rocks, formed from the red and orange rocks being cemented together by a white rock, lie near the trail. The mystery of the orange rock's origin is compounded by the question of how it was glued together in such a formation. Organ pipe cactus grows abundantly along this section of the trail. There are so many plants, with some of such a large size, that it looks like a cacti forest.

At each organ pipe, saguaro, and cholla cacti, have the children take a close look for dead branches where all the flesh has decayed. Can they notice the difference between the underlying wood of each cactus type? A cholla skeleton looks like a mesh of smaller fibers woven together in a regular pattern. A saguaro is held together by strong, rope-like cords that run the length of the cactus and are far apart from each other. The wood under an organ pipe branch is like a large, hollow tube. Close inspection shows tiny holes at regular intervals along the surface. Although each skeleton is different, each is light-weight and very strong to support the gallons of water stored in its flesh after a rain.

By the wash at 1 mile, the organ pipe growth is once more spread out. As you cross the wash, see if the children notice the large-grain sand in its bottom. Its copper color is different from the white, fine sand usually found, but it comes from the nearby brown, eroding rock. Just past the wash, the trail gets difficult to follow, but continue straight to a rock cairn where it once more becomes clear. At 1.25 miles, the trail reaches the top of a small hill, then descends into another flat plain where it is faint, but still visible.

Off to the right of the trail at 1.35 miles, a wire fence with danger signs surrounds the shaft of an old mine. The opening is filled with dirt and is covered with a heavy wire screen to keep people from the perilous tunnels below. The pile of green stones left as tailings attests that the mine was once active when people searched for copper-laden malachite. Continue down the trail where, at 1.5 miles, the remains of an old metal shack lie in a state of collapse. With your back to the rusting heap, look across a deep wash to another fence surrounding another mine. The trail through the wash is clear and, at 1.6 miles, the timbers inside the second shaft are visible. As with the first mine, a strong wire fence and a metal grate directly over the shaft try to protect against the dangers below; however, this opening is not filled with dirt. Notice the scrape marks under the grate that look as though someone slid underneath to enter the mine. The risk of exploring old mining works far outweighs the reward.

Look at the piles of green stones and the concrete slab that helped in some way in the mining process, then return to the trailhead along the same path.

Organ pipe cactus

50. Senita Basin Trail

Location: Organ Pipe Cactus National Monument
Difficulty: Easy
Distance: 3-mile loop
Hiking time: 2.5 hours
Hikable: October-April
Elevation gain: 180 feet
Map: USGS Lukeville

The small mountains that form the Senita Basin are the home of the senita cactus as well as white granite; black, brown, and red volcanic rock; quartz; and spider webs encircling holes in the ground. The trail follows a roughly triangular loop route past deep, rocky washes and wisps of grass between distant clumps of desert plants. Have the children watch for the saguaro that lived through a rough childhood, and peer into the sealed shaft of a long-closed mine. The trail is suitable for children of all ages. There are no bathrooms or water at the trailhead.

Driving Instructions: From Phoenix, travel south on Interstate 10 for 31 miles to the interchange with Interstate 8. Travel west on Interstate 8 for 65 miles to State Highway 85, then proceed 66 miles south on Highway 85, past the city of Why, to the well-marked pullout for the entrance to Organ Pipe Cactus National Monument. Follow the signs to the Vistors Center, pay the entrance fee, then return to Highway 85 and continue south to the intersection with Puerto Blanco Road. Turn right onto the dirt Puerto Blanco Drive and continue about 3 miles to the intersection with Senita Basin Road. Turn right and follow Senita Basin Road to its terminus, elevation 1,680 feet. The trailhead is well marked.

Almost immediately, the trail, marked by wooden stakes pounded into the ground and painted white on top, enters a sandy wash. Saguaro, paloverde, and silver cholla grow thickly along the wash's curving sides. A large white boulder close to the trail is either white granite or quartz, which is commonly found along with granite. The trail passes through a second wash, where 2-foot-high saguaro cacti grow under protective nurse plants, before arriving at a well-marked intersection, the first corner of the triangle, at 0.2 mile.

Take the left fork as it leads into a basin formed by low mountains, which provides the ideal climate for the senita cactus to thrive. Both the organ pipe and senita cacti grow in clumps, but an observant eye can detect larger pleats in the senita arms and thick patches of gray needles at the ends of older senita plants. Cacti of both types grow next to the trail, so have the children watch closely to discover the first senita cactus along the way.

The route continues over small, rolling hills through and past sometimes deep washes. With the children, look at the numerous and varied footprints in the sandy sections of the trail. Search for any animal tracks. Although the trail is well defined, white stakes occasionally mark the way, while small, white, quartz-like stones lie embedded under foot. The color of the granite rocks and sand ranges from gray to brown to a reddish rose tint.

An intersection in the wide wash at 0.4 mile would be confusing if it were not for the many rock cairns indicating the right direction. The landscape, especially when viewed from a distance, appears green and filled with plant life; however, a closer look reveals large plants, such as saguaro, organ pipe cacti, ocotillo, and paloverde, growing in tight clumps separated by stretches of sparse, green grass.

At 0.9 mile, patches of dark volcanic rock are a prelude to a small hill of the same material. The dark stone is from lava, which is an extrusive volcanic stone because it pushed out of the magma chamber and then cooled; whereas the granite formed as magma solidified underground and is called intrusive volcanic rock. Granite is later exposed through erosion.

The next intersection, the second corner of the triangle, lies just beyond the small brown hill. Take the 270-degree right turn to follow the trail past small holes in the ground surrounded by spider webs waiting to catch unsuspecting insects like crickets. Have children watch also for lizards that scurry down larger holes under bushes. Washes run alongside the trail, sometimes winding toward and then away.

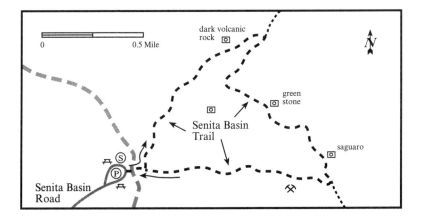

The white stake at 1.25 miles marks the trail just before it descends into the wash that paralleled the right side of the trail. At 1.35 miles, two saguaro cacti grow from the same root system and by 1.6 miles, rust-red rocks lie strewn around the ground. Just 0.1 mile later, the red rocks give way to green ones, which cover the ground for the next several tenths of a mile.

See if the children can watch for cholla cacti that have lost their joints. Cholla spreads when a joint from a plant breaks off and takes root. It would seem that the joints would fall directly from the plant to the ground, but notice that a plant 3 feet in diameter is surrounded by a circle of joints that is 6 feet around because the falling segments bounce and roll on impact.

The wash at 1.9 miles marks the location of the saguaro that had a rough childhood. While leaving the wash, have the children look at the 10-foot-tall saguaro with three constriction marks with large bulges in between. How do they suppose the cactus got this way? Each narrow band is a sign of a cold winter where the plant froze. The bulges show that there were good years between freezes and no cold winters since the three that left their marks.

The last corner of the triangle lies just past the saguaro, at 1.95 miles. Take the sharp right turn to continue along the trail. Senita Basin is formed by low-lying, rounded mountains, but behind them rise pointed, rough volcanic peaks. At 2.2 miles, on the left is a mine shaft encircled by a protective fence that has been filled with dirt. The trail follows a slight descent past ocotillo that has red blossoms in the spring, back to the original corner of the triangle at 2.8 miles.

Continue straight, ignoring the sharp right turn, to recross the first, wide wash back to the trailhead.

Appendix
Land Management Agencies

Grand Canyon National Park
P.O. Box 129
Grand Canyon, AZ 86023
(520) 638-7779
Hikes: 1, Bright Angel Point Trail; 2, Cape Royal Trail;
3, Cliff Spring Trail

Navajo National Monument
HC 71, Box 3
Tonalea, AZ 86044-9704
(520) 672-2366 or 672-2367
Hikes: 4, Sandal Trail; 5, Aspen Forest Overlook Trail;
6, Betatakin Trail

Wupatki and Sunset Crater Volcano National Monument
2717 North Steves Boulevard, Suite 3
Flagstaff, AZ 86004
(520) 556-7152
Hikes: 7, Lava Flow Nature Trail; 8, Wukoki and Wupatki Ruins;
9, Doney Mountain Trail

Peaks Ranger District
5075 North Highway 89
Flagstaff, AZ 86004
(520) 526-0866
Hikes: 10, Lava River Cave; 11, Viet Springs Trail; 13, Red Mountain
Trail; 14, Sunset Trail; 16, Ledges Trail

Tusayan Ranger District
P.O. Box 3088
Grand Canyon, AZ 86023
(520) 638-2443
Hike: 12, Red Butte Trail

Walnut Canyon National Monument
Walnut Canyon Road
Flagstaff, AZ 86004
(520) 526-3367
Hike: 15, Island Trail

Sedona Ranger District
P.O. Box 300
Sedona, AZ 86339
(520) 282-4119
Hike: 17, Devils Bridge

Tonto Natural Bridge State Park
P.O. Box 1245
Payson, AZ 85547
(520) 476-4202
Hikes: 18, Gowan Loop Trail; 19, Pine Creek Trail

Mesa Ranger District
P.O. Box 5800
Mesa, AZ 85211-5800
(602) 379-6446
Hikes: 20, Boulder Canyon Trail; 21, Second Water Trail;
    22, Dutchmans–Bluff Spring Trails Loop

Maricopa County Parks and Recreation Department
3475 West Durango Street
Phoenix, AZ 85009
(602) 506-2930
Hikes: 23, Lousley Hill Trail; 25, Pass Mountain Trail;
    26, Merkle and Vista Trails

Phoenix Parks Department
200 West Washington, 16th floor
Phoenix, AZ 85003
(602) 262-6862
Hikes: 24, Lookout Mountain Circumference Trail; 27, Camelback
    Summit Trail; 28, North Mountain National Trail

Santa Catalina Ranger District
5700 North Sabino Canyon Road
Tucson, AZ 85750
(520) 749-8700
Hikes: 29, Molino Trail; 30, Sycamore Reservoir Trail; 31,
    Mount Lemmon and Lemmon Rock Lookout Trails; 32, Mount
    Lemmon, Lemmon Rock Lookout, and Wilderness of Rocks
    Trails; 33, Incinerator Ridge Trail; 34, Mount Bigelow Trail;
    35, Butterfly Peak; 36, Butterfly Trail; 37, Crystal Spring
    Trail

Saguaro National Park
3693 South Old Spanish Trail
Tucson, AZ 85730
(520) 733-5158
Hikes: 38, Valley View Overlook Trail; 39, Signal Hill Trail

Arizona State Parks
1300 West Washington
Phoenix, AZ 85007
(602) 542-4174
Hike: 40, Hunter Trail

Coronado National Memorial
4101 East Montezuma Canyon Road
Hereford, AZ 85615
(520) 366-5515
Hikes: 41, Coronado Cave Trail; 42, Coronado Peak Trail

Chiricahua National Monument
HCR 2, Box 6500
Willcox, AZ 85643
(520) 824-3560
Hikes: 43, Echo Canyon and Hailstone Trails; 44, Sugarloaf
    Mountain Trail; 45, Massai Point Nature Trail

Nogales Ranger District
303 Old Tucson Road
Nogales, AZ 85621
(520) 281-2296
Hikes: 46, Dutch John Spring Trail; 47, Madera Canyon Nature
    Trail

Organ Pipe Cactus National Monument
Route 1, Box 100
Ajo, AZ 85321
(520) 387-6849
Hikes: 48, Red Tanks Tinaja Trail; 49, Dripping Springs Mine
    Trail; 50, Senita Basin Trail

Suggested Reading

Carline, and Lentz, Macdonald. *Mountaineering First Aid: A Guide to Accident Response and First Aid Care*. Seattle: The Mountaineers, 1996.

Chronic, Halka. *Roadside Geology of Arizona*. Missoula, Mont.: Mountain Press Publishing, 1983.

Epple, Anne Orth. *A Field Guide to the Plants of Arizona*. Helena, Mont.: Falcon Press Publishing, 1995.

Fleming, June. *Staying Found: The Complete Map and Compass Handbook*. Seattle: The Mountaineers, 1994.

Henry, Marguerite. *Brighty of the Grand Canyon*. New York: Aladdin Books, Macmillan Publishing Co., 1991.

Letham, Lawrence. *GPS Made Easy: Using Global Positioning Systems in the Outdoors*. Seattle: The Mountaineers, 1995.

Index

Early people used large alcoves to shelter their homes from the elements.

About the Author

Lawrence Letham received a Bachelor of Science degree from the University of Utah in 1984 and a Master of Science degree from Lehigh University in 1990. Both degrees are in the field of Electrical Engineering. He has worked in the electronics industry since 1984 designing integrated circuits, those tiny chips that make our electronic gadgets increasingly powerful and inexpensive. He has also done some software development.

Lawrence discovered the outdoors as a boy scout at age 12 and has hiked and camped ever since. As an adult, he has found that the outdoors takes on new meaning when experienced with children because simple things like insects, leaves, and rocks become objects of profound wonder. One of his favorite activities is to explore new areas with his wife and six children. They have lived on both east and west coasts of the United States and in several states in between, which has provided them the opportunity to see and enjoy many different areas, climates, and cultures. They now live in Arizona and find its outdoor wonders exciting to discover. Lawrence is also the author of the book *GPS Made Easy: Using Global Positioning Systems in the Outdoors,* also published by the Mountaineers.